SESSIONS WITH MATTHEW

Smyth & Helwys Publishing, Inc.
6316 Peake Road
Macon, Georgia 31210-3960
1-800-747-3016
© 2008 by Smyth & Helwys Publishing
All rights reserved.
Printed in the United States of America.

Library of Congress Cataloging-in-Publication Data

Shiell, William David, 1972–
Sessions with Matthew / William D. Shiell.
p. cm.
Includes bibliographical references and index.
ISBN 978-1-57312-501-7
1. Bible. N.T. Matthew—Criticism, interpretation, etc. I. Title.

BS2575.52.S39 2008
226.2'07—dc22

2007042263

Sessions *with*
Matthew

● ● ● Becoming a *Family*
of *Faith*

William D. Shiell

SMYTH&HELWYS
PUBLISHING, INCORPORATED • MACON, GEORGIA

Dedication

To my mother, Sara Shiell.
Since 1979, she has told the story of Jesus' life through
word and deed to the first grade Sunday school of
First Baptist Church, Pensacola, Florida.

Acknowledgments

I am so grateful to Drs. Mikeal Parsons, Naymond Keathley, and Charles Talbert for teaching me to read the New Testament from the perspective of the first-century audience. Their insights and the opportunity to grade movie reviews for Dr. Keathley's "Life and Teachings of Christ" planted the seeds that have borne fruit in this project.

This book would not be possible without the support of my wife, Kelly, our son Parker, and the newest addition to our family, Drake, who entered this world when I finished the manuscript. Thank you to Michael McCullar and Keith Gammons for inviting me to be a part of this series. I am grateful to the gracious listeners of First Baptist Church, Knoxville, Tennessee, who are hearers and doers of the Word. Harold Julian and Ross Brummett have provided excellent editorial suggestions. I am especially grateful to the "guinea pigs" of the Dunbarton Oaks Men's Bible Study group who heard the first drafts, offered ideas, asked great questions, and provided helpful insights.

—Easter 2007

Table of Contents

Introducing Matthew

Imagine that the year is AD 85. The Romans have crushed Jerusalem so badly that they destroyed the temple. Jewish friends are devastated. The homeland is gone; all of Jesus' predictions have been fulfilled, except one. He has not yet returned. Eyewitnesses have died. The younger generations do not know the stories as the elders do. Various versions of Jesus' message circulate, some contradicting others. Few written records exist because most people expected Jesus to return by now.

In Antioch, believers in Jesus' resurrection gather in the small meeting place for a meal. The leader of the group announces that he has a surprise. Following the meal, instead of the usual musical entertainment and readings from the Hebrew Scripture, he holds up a scroll just delivered from a slave in a nearby community. The group gathers, and people rejoice because they hear great news. The scroll begins, "The book of the genealogy of Jesus Christ . . . ."

This scenario of an early reading of the Gospel of Matthew paints a picture of what life could have been like in the early days of the church. Stress and worry pervaded the band of believers. They had few written records of Jesus' life, and the only one known to exist at the time was the Gospel of Mark. Then an anonymous writer penned another volume, another version of Jesus' life. We know it today as the Gospel of Matthew.

The first Gospel, and the first book of the New Testament, is an ancient biography of the founder of Christianity. The book of Matthew follows the conventions of ancient biographies such as Plutarch's *Parallel Lives*, Suetonius's *Lives of the Caesars*, and Josephus's *Life*.

In the past, Christian scholars have said that the Gospels were unique, that the New Testament writers "invented" the genre of Gospel, or that no one wrote quite like the writers of the Gospels. No work in the ancient or modern world exists in a vacuum, however. God did not dictate the words, and the Gospel writers were not secluded on a desert island as they wrote. Like all works of literature, the book of Matthew contains unique features. New Testament Gospels follow the form, however, of other literary works from their day in the genre of *bioi* or biographies. Similar to other biographies in the ancient world, Matthew describes Jesus' family origins, teachings, followers, and actions. It paints a picture for those who want to know more about them, entertains the listeners as post-dinner entertainment, informs their belief in Jesus, shows them how to imitate his actions in society, and gives them material for retelling the story to others.

Modern biographies such as David McCullough's narrative *John Adams* or Debby Applegate's story of Henry Ward Beecher, *The Most Famous Man in America*, recount the key events of the central figure in chronological sequence. They set the figure within his context, discuss in detail other historical events at the time, and note how the figure related to other events in the world. The conclusion summarizes the key themes of life. An individual reads the book silently and might discuss the work in a book club or class.

By contrast, ancient biographies were written more for their persuasive, entertainment, or, in the case of Matthew, theological value rather than as historical chronology. Ancient writers seem to care little about time lines and sequence. They wrote for audiences to respond to the memorable figure. Their works were read following dinner parties to entertain and inform guests.

The closest analogies we have in modern society are episodes of A&E's *Biography* series or a profile of a historic figure on the Biography Channel. People watch to learn more about a person and potentially emulate their lives, and the episodes offer entertainment and educational value.

In the ancient world, the oral biographies read by a slave lector provided post-dinner conversation and entertainment for a culture familiar with Greco-Roman theater. The audience could jeer, laugh, applaud, and participate in the experience. The reader could use others to act like a Greco-Roman chorus and could portray the characters in the narrative like actors in a play.

What makes Matthew unique is the effect the central figure had on others: Jesus was born, lived, died, and was resurrected. The followers of Jesus responded to this message by faith and shared it, changing the world.

In this study of Matthew, we will attempt to answer the questions that any first-century listener would have asked about the person of Jesus in a biography: Who was related to Jesus? What happened when he was born? What did he say? Who followed him? What did he do? How did he die? What happened after he died? To answer the questions, we will attempt to immerse ourselves in the first-century world so that we can understand Matthew's work from an ancient perspective. What the text meant to the original audience will give us clues about what it means to us today.

In each study, we will discuss how an ancient listener understood the passage before approaching the modern context. We will also focus on passages unique to Matthew. Unlike some studies that compare Matthew's version of events with other Gospels, we will focus on passages that make Matthew unique. For instance, Matthew's Sermon on the Mount and Luke's Sermon on the Plain are similar, but Matthew cannot be understood without reading the Sermon on the Mount in its final form.

Like citizens of the ancient world, we worry about the future and encounter people who claim to know the story of Jesus but who portray a different and perhaps unfamiliar version. Because of the multiplicity of churches and beliefs about Jesus, we need to be better informed. Our understanding of who we worship affects how we live. Our perspective of Jesus' family, teachings, followers, and actions informs what we believe about him, how we live like him, and how we talk about him to others.

So that we may learn more about the most important person who ever lived, this study will help us read Matthew in light of the listeners' expectations and hopes and will draw analogies to the modern world. Prepare to read this study by taking time to read the sections of the Gospel aloud and hear them as the early listeners did. Read each section a few times with vocal inflection. Imagine the characters coming alive for the first time. Put yourself in the hearers' places, and learn again who Jesus is, the One who is at the center of Matthew's family of faith.

P a r t I

Jesus' Life

An ancient biography described the birth of a significant figure, sometimes noting a divine origin, and included his significant family ties. The biography featured major teachings, actions, and characters who emulated the central figure.

In this first section of the study of Matthew, we will trace these similar themes through the first 20 chapters of the book. I have arranged this section to address these themes in the narrative order in Matthew. First, we discuss his family ties and genealogy. The people in Matthew's genealogy of Jesus provide significant clues to the scope of Jesus' life and ministry. Second, we turn to the supernatural, natural, and tragic events surrounding his birth. In sessions 3–5, we will look at his teachings from the Sermon on the Mount, the followers who were first attracted to him, and significant miracles he performed. We will save the discussion of the parables for section 2. A careful reader of Matthew knows that we can find teachings interspersed among the descriptions of followers and miracles. Some Bible studies choose to address everything Jesus said on a certain topic in Matthew under one heading. These studies, however, miss the narrative arrangement of the book in its final form. They miss the opportunity to view the book as one that was to be read and performed orally.

Matthew has been received by the church in this sequence and is read as part of worship. By reading the Gospel in the arrangement as we have it, we preserve its narrative quality as a biography of Jesus. We have a chance to hear it read as the first listeners might have understood the book. We can listen for the overall sense of the narrative and decide how we might respond in our time.

Who Were Jesus' Ancestors?

Matthew 1:1-25
Focal text—Matthew 1:1-25

Family histories come in all shapes and sizes. We go to great trouble to preserve what we know. Some people collect photos in albums that yellow with age and use. My wife enjoys clipping pictures and recording data in scrapbooks on acid-free paper. Computer software and the Internet provide access to genealogical data to complete the puzzle of missing names, faces, and locations. A few families have even gone to the trouble of publishing a historical record.

We remember a person's family history because it tells us something about him. A person is identified with a certain set of people; he passes along values, ideas, and concepts through the family system. When we know an individual's family, we think we understand him better and can form a better picture of the person.

Matthew's Gospel opens with a list of fascinating characters. It's more than a genealogy. The list provides an oral history of names and faces that prepare the reader to meet the Son of God. When we know a bit about Jesus' family, we are better prepared to understand the significance of his life.

Matthew's Genealogy of Jesus

In our world, family histories are usually passed from one generation to another orally and visually. When people are added to the family at births or weddings and when we say goodbye at funerals, family histories are told: "He looks just like Grandpa." "She has your eyes." "He acts just like your uncle did at that age." "I hope he treats her better than he treated his first wife." "She could make pot pie better than anyone."

Simple statements are spoken at significant milestones, and they point to a story behind the person. People remember the characters who stand out. We recall the ones with the sordid pasts and those we loved the most. Depending on who tells the story, some characters are omitted and others embellished. These are the scenes shared late at night at the family reunion after the children have gone to bed. They are the incidents related at a funeral when memories offer a soothing balm or a doorway into the "truth."

The ancient world also shared biographical data orally and visually. With few written family records, history was shared from one person to another. Ancient biographies such as Plutarch's *Parallel Lives* and Suetonius's *Lives of the Caesars* contained a particular kind of family tree. Like a photo album or scrapbook, the genealogy connected the person to the past and to certain historical figures (Quintilian, *Inst. Or.* 3.7.10). The list gave the central character credibility, revealed certain things about him, and prepared the reader for events in his life.

Visual elements complemented the stories. Vases, jars, cups, and walls were filled with pictures of famous and infamous figures that were significant to a household or culture. For instance, in Dura-Europas, an ancient Syrian village, archaeologists discovered a synagogue and a church dating from the third century AD that contained mosaics. They showed images of Moses and the burning bush, the children of Israel destroying their gold, and Ezekiel and the valley of dry bones. The church walls were filled with Old Testament scenes and depictions of Jesus' life. They offered a historical "photo album" for all to see.

Matthew's biography fits this oral-visual culture. The Gospel is more than news about Jesus' life. It's the "genesis," a term used in 1:1, to describe Jesus' beginnings and the start of a new way of living. His story takes on more meaning because the opening chapter introduces his life and because the characters are linked theologically to the larger story of God's redemptive work. It's a biography of how faithful and unfaithful past lives are linked to one significant life. Jesus founded a new movement—a new way of living—that became the church.

Imagine the effect this genealogy had on Matthew's congregation. They were likely located in Antioch around AD 85, fifteen years after the fall of the Jerusalem temple. This gathering of mainly Jewish and some Gentile believers heard not only Jesus' story, but also the story of how their lives were part of God's work in the world. The characters from the past listed in the ancient genealogy are like the photos in the album worth preserving, but they are more than that. As in the stories told at the birth of a child (and later at death), certain characters are brought to mind who are validated because Jesus lived. They might have been scorned in the past, but his life makes their lives mean something. Some people long forgotten are now part of the collective family of Jesus.

Matthew's biography could have had a visual element to it. We do not have an example of pictures to accompany the stories of Jesus, but one hypothetical scenario is that some of the characters mentioned might have been painted on the walls of a church like that in Dura-Europas. At the least, their reputations were easily recalled as listeners heard the names recited.

With this in mind, the genealogy that opens Jesus' biography contains many possibilities. Each character mentioned is connected to Jesus' family and had meaning for the listeners who simply wanted to know who was related to Jesus. Each individual's relationship to Jesus changed the way the church shared the message of Jesus with their culture.

A PICTURE OF JESUS' FAMILY (1:1-17)

As with any other genealogy in the ancient world, Matthew does not include everyone related biologically to Jesus. His is a theological list rather than a family tree, so the list contains the significant names for Matthew's purposes that reflect a certain picture of Jesus. There are people in Jesus' background who indicate the kind of life he leads, the ministry he performs, and the values he shares.

This genealogy is divided into three groups. The first is a group of eighteen names with fourteen generations from Abraham to Jesse. The second is a group of sixteen names with fourteen generations from David to the Babylonian exile. The third is a group of fifteen names with thirteen generations from Jechoniah to Jesus.

Abraham	David, *wife* of Uriah	Jechoniah
Isaac	Solomon	Shealtiel
Jacob	*Rehoboam*	Zerubbabel
Judah and *brothers*	Abijah	Abiud
Perez, *Tamar*	Asa	Eliakim
Zerah	Jehoshaphat	Azor
Hezron	Joram	Zadok
Ram	Uzziah	Achim
Amminadab	Jotham	Eliud
Nahshon	Ahaz	Eleazar
Salmon, *Rahab*	Hezekiah	Matthan
Boaz, *Ruth*	*Manasseh*	Jacob
Obed	Amos	*Mary*, Joseph
Jesse	Josiah	Jesus called Christ
David	Jechoniah and *brothers*	

Some ancient biographies linked people to noble ancestry. Some also indicated that one could demonstrate success from meager circumstances (Theon, *Rhetorical Handbook* 110-112). Matthew does both. He links Jesus to David by grouping the first two lists in sections of fourteen, the numerical equivalent in Hebrew to the name "David." Three categories reveal his humble beginnings: mothers, brothers, and sinners.

The mothers. Matthew mentions five women in these verses: Tamar (v. 3), Rahab (v. 5), Ruth (v. 5), "the wife of Uriah" (v. 6), and Mary (v. 16). These women share several characteristics. Their marriages were unconventional. Tamar joined the family of Judah in Genesis 38 when Judah arranged for his son Er to marry her. When Er died and his brother did not perform his duty under levirate tradition (Gen 38:9), Tamar disguised herself as a prostitute, covered her face, and became the mother of Judah's offspring (Gen 38:26). Rahab did not disguise herself as a prostitute; she was one (Josh 7:1). Ruth entered the city of Bethlehem as a widow and a pagan Moabitess before marrying Boaz (Ruth 3:10-11). Bathsheba's name is not even mentioned here, but most people in Matthew's day understood the reference to Uriah, just as believers do today (2 Sam 11:11). Mary, Jesus' mother, entered marriage with the stigma of an unplanned pregnancy. In the genealogy, she receives a prominent place. Joseph is listed as the "husband of Mary," rather than the expected description, "father of Jesus."

The brothers. Another group that plays a key role in the genealogy is the "brothers." In the first two groups of generations, the "brothers" of individuals are noted. Verse 2 references the brothers of Judah, the other eleven leaders of the tribes of Israel. Verse 11 mentions the brothers of Jechoniah (1 Chr 3:15).

The sinners. Sinners also play key roles in this genealogy. One would expect prominent, upstanding men to be featured in most ancient records. Instead, some of the worst are mentioned. The five women are not the only ones who arise from questionable circumstances. Many of the men have sordid pasts. For instance, Manasseh (v. 10) was one of the worst kings in all of Israel (2 Kgs 21:1-18). He inherited the throne from one of the most respected kings in Judah, his father, Hezekiah. He disgraced his family by leading the people into more evil practices than those committed by the nations surrounding Judah (Garland, *Reading Matthew*, 18).

THE NEW BEGINNING (1:18-25)

The family portrait becomes even more significant in light of the circumstances surrounding the birth. A young thirteen- or fourteen-year-old single girl had been told by her parents that she would marry a carpenter named Joseph. Their system of arranged marriages did not allow for modern notions of courtship. Families gave away daughters in exchange for money to another family connected to the clan.

There were no blind dates for the young teenager and her righteous husband Joseph. They did not fall in love; love would come later after the commitment. During the engagement or "betrothal," Mary would live with Joseph's family for a period of six months to a year while the wedding plans were made. Mary's father gave a gift called a dowry for allowing Mary to become engaged to Joseph. Depending on the abilities of Joseph's family, they too would return a small gift to the bride's family.

The parents had everything planned, but a miraculous conception changed the plans. Mary noticed something. Her body was changing; things were not quite right this month. Perhaps she went to her mom to get advice. When the moment came, she would have to tell Joseph the worst news of all—she was pregnant. Imagine the look of horror, the surprise, the shock. In her mind, she might have asked, "How can it be? We barely know each other. I'm pure. I try my best to follow God's laws."

Everyone could also hear the whispers, made more audible by the centuries of family dysfunction in the house of Joseph, the same whispers they heard about Tamar committing adultery; the same kinds of acts of immorality Manasseh allowed to ruin the country; the same activities Rahab engaged in; and now Joseph and Mary. The Nazareth whisperers figured these two from Galilee were no different; they were all the same. "History repeats itself." "The sins of the fathers reaped on the fourth generation." "You know how it is with the young people of this generation." "What we need to do is get rid of them." "They don't treat adulterers today like they used to."

Right before the gossipers and the "holier-than-thous" pronounced Joseph and Mary guilty before proven innocent, a little phrase marks a new beginning.

The true meaning of verse 18 is "beginnings." The word used here is from the same root as the word "genesis." This is how the birth or the beginning of Jesus took place. It is more than a simple phrase to end a genealogy. The statement includes everything that has taken place up to this time in the world. The writer of the Gospel of Matthew says, "What we need here is a new beginning. This world is headed downward in a hurry. Even the lawgivers and the obedient ones cannot follow the law; the whole system is broken."

The family of Joseph looked at the family tree and said the seeds of dysfunction were also the beginnings of a new creation. They had been there with Tamar and Manasseh; they'd seen what could happen when things got out of hand. And in one moment things began to change. In one angelic visit, God changed the way people thought about Joseph's family and all the families of the world.

Prior to this time, the gossipers and whisperers were right. We can imagine that each time they told Tamar's and Mannasseh's stories, they found a parallel story in their own time. As they shared the stories across generations, Joseph's family appeared to repeat a cycle of dysfunction.

With a new beginning, however, everything changes. Now the family of Joseph looke at the family tree and said that the seeds of dysfunction are also the beginning of a new creation. In one angelic visit, God changed the way people think about Joseph's family and all the families of the world. Previous seeds sown with misdeeds and dysfunction can become fertile soil through the life-giving birth of Jesus.

God signified this change through the words of the angel, who spoke to Joseph in a dream:

(1) "Do not fear" (1:20). Fear causes you to withdraw and listen to the whispers from the family tree. Move through the fear and continue the betrothal.

(2) "This is my responsibility" (1:20-22). God is responsible for the pregnancy; Joseph can be responsible for being faithful to Mary.

(3) "Name the child" (1:23). Call him Jesus, the Greek equivalent of the Hebrew "Yeshua." Isaiah's hopes will be fulfilled. Because a virgin experiences a miraculous conception, God has not abandoned the world. This child Immanuel offers a testimony of something that God wants people to remember about Joseph's family—"God with us."

In one moment, God changed everything for Joseph.

Think about what "God with us" meant for Joseph's past. He could look at his own family tree and see Tamar, Rahab, Manasseh, Ruth, and other people the gossipers whispered about. But God said throughout the family history and in their history, "I am with you always."

God may not have liked their decisions, but he worked through their sinfulness, taking their shameful conduct and leading to this point of new beginnings. God did not reject the family because of their choices.

Joseph was able to look at his present circumstances and say, "We do not have to be ashamed of what is happening now. We can still trust in God to get us through the unknowns of our lives."

In an understated way, the text says Joseph woke up and did what the angel commanded. The next time we meet the family, they are forced to flee because of the king, and their faith in "God with us" is put to the test.

The Significance of the Genealogy

Jesus' family album speaks volumes about his life and ministry and evokes radical images. His ministry built relationships with people who disobeyed God's law and who were abandoned by God's people. The immoral, repugnant, rejected, religious, and political fill the list. This list was merely a starting point for Jesus' life and ministry. The genealogy forms a template for reaching out to people with sinful reputations and welcoming them into a spiritual family.

By looking into Jesus' past, we anticipate who will be associated with his ministry family.

One group is omitted, however. In verse 17, Matthew mentions fourteen generations "from the deportation to Babylon to the Messiah," but only thirteen are actually listed in verses 12-16. Could Matthew's church be the missing fourteenth generation (Garland, *Reading Matthew*, 19)?

In Matthew's day, the church was filled with noble and ignoble characters. Jews and Gentiles populated the region around Antioch. They identified with the characters in the story. They knew their lives were like those of the people in the past. None of them deserved to be in the family, but Jesus welcomed all of them.

Jesus' Faith Family Today

The genealogy indicates that Jesus' birth created a new definition of family. People are related to one another spiritually through their connection to Jesus. He makes a spiritual faith family, not one tied together through bloodlines or ethnicity. He creates an opportunity for a new relationship with God despite sinful deeds in the past or reputations in the community.

The church of today continues the faith family—for good or bad. We are part of the fourteenth generation. Positively, many in church have been welcomed because they are misfits in society. Many people identify their church as "home"; they sing that they are in "the family of God," and in some traditions they refer to each other as "brother" or "sister."

The old Bill Gaither lyrics reflect this sentiment:

I'm so glad I'm a part of the family of God
I've been washed in the fountain,
Cleansed by his blood,
Joint heirs with Jesus as we travel this sod,
For I'm part of the family, the family of God.

Churches understand that a relationship with God cannot be passed through bloodlines. Individuals must respond to Jesus' invitation personally. We cannot exclude people based on race or gender; we invite all God's children to come.

Compare Jesus' family tree, however, to a roll call in most churches. The "family of God" looks fairly normal on the outside. Are there really that many people like the wife of Uriah? How many people have the reputation of Manasseh? If Jesus' family tree were used as a template for measuring success, most churches would fall painfully short.

Where to begin? We can begin with our family of origin. Jesus' family includes the scandalized (Manasseh), the tawdry (Tamar), the Gentile (Ruth), the frightened (Mary and Joseph). He uses ordinary and less-than-desirable people as the foundation on which he can build a new kind of family. A new generation of believers is born through the coming of the Messiah/Christ. When his history is recorded, people will know that God has been with them (v. 23).

Most families experience some sort of dysfunction. The photo album is the best place to identify people who need the love of Christ. The people who appear only at weddings and funerals can become the starting point for new relationships. When other members of the family are rejected because of their sinful behavior, the faith family finds a way to associate with them, following the pattern of Jesus' genealogy. Matthew's genealogy gives the church a list of qualities and characteristics of people who need the love of Christ.

Another place to find them is at the family reunion meal. Joseph calls out to us from the dinner table and says, "Look at my family; I've got them, too. And God is still with us." We discover this promise when we look at our own Tamars and Manassehs, Rahabs and Ruths, Marys and Josephs and say "God is with us." God may not like their behavior, but God also has not enjoyed how others have treated them. In God's eyes, everyone is equal, and God is equally with all of his creation.

One church attempted to demonstrate this kind of love to Ben and Susan Thompson. In their small rural community, everyone knew everybody else's business, and most of it was gossip about Ben and Susan. As teenagers they were active in their respective churches, but while they were dating in high school, Susan became pregnant.

Following their marriage and birth of the baby, Susan joined Ben's church, and they remained active members for a while. She eventually gave birth to another baby, and Ben and Susan had a happy marriage, family, and church life until the kids became teenagers. At that point the Thompsons decided to adopt an African-American girl and a Caucasian boy.

Despite integration of the public schools, the Thompsons' community was still largely segregated geographically and economically, so its response to an interracial adoption was not wholly unpredictable. It was no surprise when someone in the church made a racist remark to the couple.

The church ignored the comment, but the Thompsons did not. Ben's family of origin did not confront the issue but allowed the church member to go unchecked and Ben and his family to withdraw into the safe confines of their house.

Barriers like these are not mended easily. During the week, people saw the family at the grocery store and baseball games. In the summer, the family surfaced for the occasional wedding. At the funeral home, Ben and Susan attended as faithful friends and supporters. But they would not attend the church, and the church talked about Ben, Susan, and the kids as if the Thompsons were no longer a part of the faith family.

An honest look at the church's membership revealed something, however. It was full of misfits, of people who had long ignored a series of misdeeds and misbehaviors. But how could they repair damage caused over the years by harsh words? The church found an entry point during a crisis. Ben needed surgery, and the church offered to provide meals. It was a small gesture, but the church's offer and the couple's response spoke volumes about both parties' willingness to reconcile. Both had done things wrongly in the past; both were willing to forgive; both were willing to reunite the spiritual family. After a long, slow, methodical process of demonstrating love to one another through word and deed, Ben and Susan—along with their biological and adopted children—reunited with the church. The faith family was reconnected. With a new understanding of grace, the church members began to see themselves as no better than anyone else and to see people of all races and backgrounds as equals in God's eyes.

This church discovered in the background of Jesus people who were like them. Those to whom they reached out discovered welcoming arms when they understood the makeup of the faith family. When both parties reconciled, together they added new pictures and wrote new chapters in the story of Jesus' family.

1. Instead of deciding what each passage in Matthew means to us, this study discusses each passage in light of its ancient meaning first. How does studying the book from the perspective of the ancient world affect interpretation today?

_____
_____
_____
_____
_____
_____

2. Matthew's biography is one of four books in the New Testament that give us a portrait of Jesus. What does the genealogy reveal about the contours of Matthew's picture of Jesus?

_____
_____
_____
_____
_____
_____

3. What are the qualifications to join Jesus' family?

_____
_____
_____
_____
_____
_____

4. Which people mentioned in Jesus' genealogy could easily fit in the hall of shame rather than the hall of fame?

_____
_____
_____
_____
_____
_____

5. Are there people in your family scrapbook with sketchy reputations?

_____

_____

_____

_____

_____

_____

6. What does Jesus' family tree teach us about treating people in our biological families?

_____

_____

_____

_____

_____

_____

7. Church, the faith family, is always filled with a variety of colorful characters. Does Jesus' family reflect your church family? Why or why not?

_____

_____

_____

_____

_____

_____

8. Church is often called a "family of faith," but it is neither a family by the standards of society nor of the Bible. What does it mean to be a "church/spiritual family"? How could the term "family" seem offensive to some? What can be done to include everyone in the group that surrounds Christ?

_____

_____

_____

_____

_____

9. Watch this scene from *The Nativity Story* DVD: chapter 12, 46:00–49:34, "Joseph's Dream" (dir. Catherine Hardwicke, Los Angeles, New Line Entertainment, 2007). How does the portrayal in the movie compare with the text in Matthew?

_____

_____

_____

_____

_____

_____

What Happened after Jesus Was Born?

Session

Matthew 1–4
Focal text—Matthew 2:1-2:24

Since September 11, 2001, traveling has not been the same. Just as surely as our leaders will continue to announce color-coded terror alerts, going through security at airports will be more time-consuming all across the country. I lived in San Angelo, Texas, during the terrorist attacks. When the FAA tightened security, San Angelo International Airport was on the frontlines of security. Security was tightly enforced, but resources were thin.

For Thanksgiving 2001, I planned to fly to Kentucky to join my wife's family for her dad's retirement celebration. My plans changed when a West Texas winter arrived early. Snow fell, and ice covered the roads. I arrived early to get through security in San Angelo. They had a unique way of stretching an hour-long process into two hours.

When I arrived at 5:10 A.M. for a 7:00 flight, the airport personnel announced that the de-icing machine was broken. They were waking the mechanic, and he was on the way. An hour later, the sleepy mechanic discovered that he did not have the right parts. The engine could not be repaired, and they needed to bring a new one from Dallas—some five hours away. Mother Nature had the last laugh, and I was stuck in the ice and snow for Thanksgiving.

My experiences were nothing compared to the travel surrounding the first public celebration of Jesus' birth 2,000 years ago. Instead of the calm, bright, silent night described in the Gospel of Luke, Matthew places the appearance of the Christ child during a season of travel, fear, hope, and salvation, all under a reign of terror by Herod the Great.

The Travelers

KING HEROD (2:1)

The first traveler in the story secured his position as king through a series of violent conquests over the villages in Palestine. He established his dominance and became known as Herod the Great. Paranoid that his power would be usurped, he moved from one place to another, overseeing his Palestinian domain that encompassed Galilee and Judea. He was a builder, constructing the seaport of Sebaste and Caesarea Maritima and beginning the construction of the Jerusalem temple. Appointed to his position of power by Mark Antony, Herod secured his authority by killing his rivals. The Romans allowed him to represent them and collect taxes from the ports and fishing revenue (Hanson and Oakman, *Palestine*, 82; Josephus, *Wars* 1.286-353).

Herod was a notorious womanizer who married ten different women. Though his was a polygamous society, Herod was not married to all ten at one time. He did, however, have several wives at once. His first wife, Doris, had only one son, Antipater. Herod sent them both into exile and married Mariamne 1. Later, Herod married Mariamne 2, mother to his favorite sons, Alexander and Aristobulus. Herod's half-sister, Salome, hated Alexander and Aristobulus even though her daughter (Bernice) had married Aristobulus. Salome wanted her own son (not her son-in-law) to succeed Herod. To this end, Salome spread rumors that Alexander and Aristobulus wanted to bring charges against Herod that would end his reign (H. W. Hoehner, "Herodian Dynasty," 317).

Paranoid and susceptible to Salome's rumors, Herod reconciled with Antipater "to show Alexander and Aristobulus that there was another heir to the throne. Antipater took full advantage of the situation and used every means to acquire the coveted throne" (Hoehner, 317). In response, Herod put Alexander and Aristobulus in prison and named Antipater heir.

Antipater, impatient to succeed his father, attempted to poison Herod, but "this plot failed when Herod's brother, Pheroras, drank the poison by mistake. Herod imprisoned Antipater and reported this attempt on his life to the emperor" (Hoehner, 318).

At this time Herod became ill with an incurable disease. He drew up a new will that bypassed his older sons, Archelaus and Philip, because Antipater had poisoned his mind against them also.

He chose his youngest son, Antipas, as his sole successor (Hanson and Oakman, 81-83).

Given the life-and-death plots for power, one can imagine why the magi's news of a new king frightened Herod (v. 3). A baby was seen as a threat to his power, and everyone knew the paranoid king was easily threatened. Herod sent the magi to continue looking for the king and asked them to send him word when they found him, ostensibly so he could greet the new king (v. 8).

THE MAGI (2:1-2)

The second travelers came from Persia. At one time, they were part of the most remarkable empires in history. The Persians had done what the Babylonians could not do—they extended Nebuchadnezzar's kingdom to Western India and modern Egypt and influenced the hearts and minds of the people. They were deeply religious. Many of them worshiped Zoroaster, a prophet who lived c. 600 BC. They believed in an afterlife and that individuals could choose their own destinies. One special group of people was at the center of their religion. They were a combination of astrologers, sorcerers, fortune-tellers, and general wise individuals, a group of men called *magoi* in Greek. The word for magi comes from the same root as our word for "magic." They were the most educated men in Persia. Their fame spread such that long after Alexander the Great defeated the Persian Empire, the magi were still around, charting the future and the stars (Brown, *Birth of the Messiah*, 167).

According to Matthew, the magi were the first to greet Jesus and the family and brought treasures of gold, frankincense, and myrrh. Scholars have wondered how the magi knew to come to the Christ child. Was it a supernatural phenomenon, Halley's comet, or Saturn and Jupiter aligning? We can date these occurrences to around this time. More likely, it was part of the mysterious plan of God that several astrologers could research, chart the heavens, and determine that they needed to arrive in the city of Jerusalem.

Their travels were not complete, however, without further direction from God (v. 12). After receiving instructions in a dream, they returned to their country by a different route to avoid the plot of Herod.

The Family (2:15-16)

After receiving the magi, the young family began a flight of escape to Egypt in the middle of the night. Matthew explains that this event fulfills a prophecy. The experience protects this family (v. 15) and destroys others (v. 16).

Herod committed infanticide on children two years and younger in the region. Given the population estimates of the day, potentially twenty-two children died because of Herod's fear. These families received no warning to leave before they suffered the loss of a child (Brown, *Birth of the Messiah*, 204).

Only Herod's death relieved the problem. According to scholars, the disease that first caused Herod to appoint an heir eventually killed him. Herod executed Antipater and altered his will. He appointed Archelaus king of Judea, Idumea, and Samaria; Antipas tetrarch of Galilee and Perea; and Philip tetrarch of territories east of Galilee. On the fifth day after Antipater's execution, in the spring of 4 BC, Herod died in Jericho. The people acclaimed Archelaus as their king, and Joseph and Mary were able to return home safely.

Their Motives

The story of Christmas is more than an idyllic porcelain manger scene placed on a mantel for all to see. As Matthew indicates, evil motives and spiritual issues lie beneath the surface. The story is incomplete without uncovering what is below. Through their behavior, the characters reveal whether they have fear, trust, or faith.

Fear Leads to Violence

Herod, a father with power to protect and a reputation to uphold, lived in fear. To preserve his power, he built fortresses and public works projects. When he heard about the most helpless of creatures, a baby, he plotted to remove the threat of Jesus. Herod, hoping to uncover another plot against himself, feigned interest in worshiping the child. He sent the magi to find the child and to report back to him. After the magi tricked Herod, he killed the firstborn children of the families in Palestine to ensure this threat against him was eliminated (Norris, *Amazing Grace*, 225-26).

The religious authorities were powerless to prevent the infanticide. They missed the importance of the star altogether. They recognized its meaning and provided the correct information, but when the king hatched his evil plan, they did nothing to stop him.

They were apparently afraid of what might happen to them if they stood up to the evil one, so they kept silent (2:4-6). TRUST LEADS TO OBEDIENCE

Joseph, ironically a father as well, had every right to be just as afraid as Herod. He, Mary, and the child were safely nestled in a house when Persian magi rode in with camels to see Jesus. The family had barely opened the presents when they found themselves on the first flight outbound to Cairo, with no express to take them there. Joseph had already risked his reputation; now his life was at stake. Armed guards searched the country for a boy not yet talking, just beginning to teethe, and perhaps taking his first few steps.

But Joseph's trust motivated him to obey God and journey to Egypt. Matthew reveals little about the journey, simply that Joseph and his family followed instructions.

FAITH LEADS TO JOY, WORSHIP, AND GENEROSITY

The magi exhibited true faith. They saw a star but did not know what it signified. Their quest resulted in joy for the star (v. 9), worship of the Christ (v. 11), and generous expressions of their devotion (v. 12).

What they lacked, however, the Jewish religious leaders had—a written record from God. Those who had the Hebrew Bible missed the miracle right in front of them. In the case of the magi, faith was more important than a written document. God used pagan astrological records and a star to point the way.

Our Response

Believers approach the message of the Christ child differently—some out of fear, others out of trust and faith. Fear is a popular response today because it motivates so much in American culture. We love to be scared—just ask amusement park operators! People spend $20 billion worldwide riding roller coasters, mostly in America (Banay, "World's Most Fun Amusement Parks"). We love the adrenaline rush of going over the edge.

People truly have not been through Matthew's story of Jesus' growth until they confront the Herod in themselves. Just as Herod was afraid, so are people today. Some avoid certain neighborhoods in fear of who lives there. Teenagers fear their parents' response to a party they attended, so they lie about where they have been. Families are afraid of what will happen in the stock market, so they do not contribute generously. Parents are afraid of what others will think about them, so they advise children not to see certain people or hang out with certain crowds. People are afraid of how their friends will perceive them, so they blend in and don't "rock the boat." Nations are afraid of people outside their borders, so they lash out at foreigners. Believers are afraid of secular people who don't celebrate Christmas in the "right" way, so they seek to impose their way on the lives of others in the public arena.

The response of fear, however, only gets us through the short term. When father Herod considered his power secure, his son Archelaus rose to the throne. Herod eliminated the infants, outwitted the magi, and allowed the natural course of events to take over. But Archelaus turned out to be a disaster. Of all the kings who reigned in the time of the Roman Empire, Archelaus served the shortest tenure. Life is more than just living out fear; that strategy proves unsuccessful in the end.

Fear can cause us to miss the miracle of Christmas. Believers need different qualities when power is stripped away and they are helpless. Four qualities are seen in the lives of the magi, Mary, and Joseph: openness to Jesus' presence on the journey, trust through the mysteries, hospitality to outsiders, and generosity to others.

INVITING JESUS ON THE JOURNEY

Matthew does not paint a picture of Jesus safely nestled in the manger. Jesus travels with Mary and Joseph on an arduous journey through the darkness. In the same way, Jesus can go with us today.

Sometimes children teach us the most about these Immanuel moments. When Randall O'Brien's youngest child, Christopher, was first learning about baby Jesus, he always wanted to take the infant out of the nativity scene and place him around the house. His family protested. Baby Jesus appeared in the bathroom. "Christopher," they said, "You can't take baby Jesus with you to the bathroom. He belongs in the manger." Very dutifully, he put the precious infant back where he belonged. The next day, once again, the baby would be taken from his safe confines of the crèche. As the family argued about where to stop to eat, they found the baby in the car. Mom and Dad confronted him: "Christopher, we can't have him in the car; he'll get lost in the car." Sunday arrived, and Christopher insisted on taking Jesus with them to church. "No, Christopher," his dad insisted, and traded a candy cane for the baby. He told Christopher, "There's too much going on in there for you to have baby Jesus with you at church" (O'Brien, *I Feel Better All Over*, 34-35).

O'Brien said Christopher was the only member of the family who did not want to leave the baby Jesus "lying in the manger." He knew the true invitation of Christmas—to take the baby everywhere the family went.

TRUSTING THROUGH THE MYSTERIES

Christmas is about putting the magic—the mysterious—back into the miracle. In so doing, we allow events that cannot be explained to become a part of our lives again. How do we explain that several rulers wandered to Jerusalem to worship a baby they had never seen? How do we understand that Joseph and Mary were in the right place at the right time to give birth to this son so that the magi could find them? How is it possible that 2,000 years later we recount the same story about men who journeyed from the east with a star to guide them? It has to be a miracle; it cannot be explained. The events call us to let the mystery remain in the miracle.

One writer has said that Christmas is a time of magic and miracle. Anyone who has directed a children's musical understands a bit about magic. After dress rehearsal, the directors think there is no way the musical will succeed. During the performance, however, a transformation occurs. The children sound like a completely different choir. That is the miracle. The magic happens when the parents look into these kids' bright faces. They do not hear wrong notes or see funny costumes; they see the potential, the spirit, and the vibrancy. When the parents' video cameras are rolling, it's like magic.

What parents see in a child's face today, magi first brought to the Christ child. They put the magic into the miracle by bringing mystery and wonder to the birth. Magi showed us that there can be a sense of wonder and awe in the world. Somehow the earthy stuff of life can be used to do the amazing, the stupendous, and the awe-inspiring.

The Jewish religious leadership missed the miracle. They should have been able to understand the sign, but they were focused more on self-preservation than on being open to new people coming into their world. Herod surrounded himself with these flatterers—these "yes" men—and they obliged him.

People can have the answers right in front of them and still miss the miracle. We can memorize Scriptures, attend dozens of services, participate in Christian activities, serve on several boards, and miss the miracle entirely. In order to see the miracle, we need the qualities that Joseph, Mary, and the magi possessed.

Their faith and trust led to obedience, joy, and worship of Christ despite their circumstances. The greatest mystery of all is why children died and Joseph and Mary fled. In Matthew, Christmas is not bright and joyful for long. There is more to the story. The first journey home for the holidays was not along the easy path, but by another route through the wilds of the desert for the magi and through Egypt for the new family. Like the sons of Israel who journeyed to Egypt to find refuge and food during a famine (Gen 42:3), so Joseph and Mary had to take their child on a difficult journey. They traveled through Roman security outposts on the frontiers of the border in Egypt, despite rumors that Herod wanted to see all the parents with infants and toddlers. They were a poorly clad couple moving to an unfamiliar place.

Families who minded their own business lost babies in the fallout of Herod's tirade. The text raises unanswerable questions. Where is their hope? Faith and trust through the mystery seem to sustain the people.

Despite the hope of the song "I'll Be Home for Christmas," sometimes people cannot go there even in their dreams. "Home" for Christmas may mean going to the desert to weep beside the grave of a loved one, to stand beside a child in the hospital and wonder how she'll survive the medication and surgery, to know that this could be the last Christmas celebrated together as a family. "Home" for thousands is to stand in the deserts of war, longing to be near loved ones. For some, it means eating alone and weeping at the kitchen table. Traveling home will never be the same.

There are probably times when we, like Mary and Joseph, have wondered, "God, aren't you going to intervene here? This is my *baby* (or mother, father, sister, brother, etc.)!" There is no intervention; there is no halt to the trials, but God continues to work in very difficult and unnatural circumstances.

Consider the story of Jennifer Audato. She was upset with God. She was twelve years old when her mother died of a brain tumor. Her constant prayers and nights at the bedside chipped away at her fragile faith instead of strengthening it. She attended a Methodist church but later dropped out. By her senior year of high school, she was participating in a Baptist church, but even then she was still angry with God. In college no one forced her to go to church; by the time she got married, Jennifer had dropped out entirely. Her husband, though, wanted God to be a part of their lives. It took a pregnancy for Jennifer to confront her own fears about God. She started attending church again and became involved in a class for new believers. She realized as a young mother that she needed to depend on God to guide her life again. After buying her first nativity set, she said, "All these years I celebrated Christmas and I was missing a major piece of the story. [God] is guiding my life now; that changes everything" (Hogan, *Dallas Morning News*).

OPENING HEARTS TO OUTSIDERS

The Jewish leadership missed an opportunity to welcome outsiders into their world. Our challenge is similar. We should ask ourselves, "Is our home big enough for these Persian magi to come?" Do we have room in our hearts and homes to extend to them the same welcome that Jesus gave? If we do not look for the outsiders and include them in our plans, we have missed the miracle of the magi.

United Methodist minister Leonard Sweet spoke at a ministers' conference in Houston about the new tasks for the church. He asked ten volunteers to form a circle. He then asked ten more and then ten more and finally ten more. Forty people formed four circles of ten each. There they stood, facing each other, feeling embarrassed and uncomfortable. He asked them if there were any other ways to form a circle. Some held hands, some locked arms around their waists. Then he asked again, "Is there any other way to form a circle?" Some of them moved in a circular pattern, some knelt, and one circle bowed toward each other. One group formed the circle facing outward.

Sweet stated, "This is the problem of the modern church. The world is in a terrible mess. And even though the gospel tells us otherwise, we form our circles, week in and week out, facing inward. We even get pretty creative about different ways to face inward, but not nearly often enough do we form our circles outward."

With his challenge in mind, I tried this at a benefit for a local homeless ministry. As part of the Bible study, I asked the group of about forty people to form circles. Following Sweet's lead, I asked them if there was any other way to form the circles. Each group turned outward, holding hands.

I congratulated them on "getting the answer right." (I confess a bit of disappointment that my illustration "worked" so quickly.) And I commended them that not only did they demonstrate the proper stance toward the community, but they held tightly to each other, indicating their unity and dependence on one another.

GENEROUSLY SHARING WITH THE WORLD

Little did the magi know that they started a tradition. When people celebrate the birth of Christ, they give gifts. The magi gave gifts to the king, celebrating his life. They took what had been given to them—the gold saved from their treasuries, the incense perhaps to be burned in their temples to false gods, the myrrh intended for burial, and, now, because they had longed for and looked for this king to come, they saw the gifts as things to be shared with the one who was coming into the world.

Mary, Joseph, and the magi knew the gift was there all along—it was the gift of this Christ child—and they knew what to do with him. They knew the gift was not to be an end in itself; the gift was to be a tool in the hands of God to change the world.

Many Christians receive gifts at Christmas. What do we do with those gifts the rest of the year? Do the gifts become another set of toys to be sold at the garage sale in a few years or upgraded to an improved version of something newer? Or will they be tools in the hands of those who know how to use them to draw others closer to Christ?

What if the toys and the gadgets, and even some of the things we needed, were transformed into a means to give others more precious gifts —like words left unspoken from the past year? The toys we received could be used to heal the hurts from a broken friendship. The computer or the X-box could be used to create a relationship with a brother or a sister who does not know Christ and needs to hear about him. The new rotisserie oven or grill could cook a turkey that could be shared with a hungry family. The guitar or the piano could be played to help others draw closer to Christ in worship. (This idea is expressed in Kyle Matthews's song, "The Gifts We Give," from the compact disc, *Timeless Christmas Child* [Nashville: See for Yourself Music, 2004]).

C. S. Lewis captures this marvelous image in his book *The Lion, the Witch, and the Wardrobe.* The children have been running from the fast-approaching white witch. They think she is on their heels, for when they look back, they see a sled. They hide in a cave, hoping they have escaped her. When the children exit the cave, they find that it is Father Christmas, or Santa Claus. He explains that Christmas has finally arrived and that the witch's power is weakening. Unloading the sleigh, he shares gifts. He gives Mrs. Beaver a new sewing machine and tells Mr. Beaver that his dam has been mended. Santa Claus then gives gifts to the children, but he tells them, "They are tools, not toys." For the coming battle, Peter receives a sword and a red shield emblazoned with a gold lion. Susan and Lucy receive gifts "to be used in time of greatest need." Susan receives a bow and arrow for defense and a horn to blow when she is in danger. Lucy receives a dagger for defense and a bottle of magic balm. A few drops can heal any ailment (Lewis, 159).

Lewis captures what the gifts of Christmas are all about. They should be tools for the difficult journey ahead. Lewis knew, as we discover in Matthew, that we are on a journey through life that involves good and bad times. But like Mary, Joseph, and the magi, with these tools and the gift of the Christ child, the journey of life will never be the same.

1. Discuss the mysteries of Matthew's story. Where did Joseph find the trust to take Mary as his wife? Why did God not halt the killings of the babies? How did the astrologers use pagan writings to discover something that the Jewish leaders had plainly in front of them?

_____
_____
_____
_____
_____
_____

2. How does fear play a role in society today? How did fear affect the reactions of the characters in Matthew? What is the difference between fear and faith?

_____
_____
_____
_____

3. Parents often use fear to motivate children. Can fear play a positive role? What are the dangers if fear is the primary motive for living?

_____
_____
_____
_____
_____
_____

4. What did you receive for Christmas two years ago? Can you remember? How have you used the gifts? What gifts have you discarded over the years?

_____
_____
_____
_____
_____
_____

5. How can the gifts you receive become tools?

_____
_____
_____
_____
_____
_____

6. What qualities did the magi demonstrate to the Christ child?

_____
_____
_____
_____
_____
_____

7. How were their attitudes different from Herod's and the religious leadership's?

_____

_____

_____

_____

_____

_____

8. Do outsiders understand the story of Christ better than people who attend church every week? Why or why not?

_____

_____

_____

_____

_____

_____

9. Watch this scene from _The Gospel according to St. Matthew_ DVD: chapter 3, 13:35–15:13 (dir. Pier Paolo Pasolini, Genius Entertainment, Legend Films, 1964, redistributed 2007). How does Pasolini's portrayal of the murder of the innocents affect your interpretation of the biblical story?

_____

_____

_____

_____

_____

What Did Jesus Say?

Matthew 5–7
Focal text—Matthew 5–7

Reading is interpreting. Unless we read to our children or listen to an audio book, reading means silently decoding words on a page and assigning them meaning in our minds. I have heard that there are a thousand ways to say "Yes," and "No," but only one way to write them down. Even Paul lamented to the Galatian believers that he wanted to be present with them so he could read the words to them himself in order to vary his tone of voice (Gal 4:19-20).

By its nature, a sermon is an oral art. Few people actually read sermon manuscripts. The homily is meant to be spoken rather than read silently, and although plenty exist in print, some listeners might wish they could read the droning message rather than hear it. Even if a preacher reads a manuscript, the hearers listen for nuance, inflection, and tone; they watch the nonverbal facial expressions and gestures.

People who study the historical Jesus and in particular the Sermon on the Mount have spent the last sixty years in critical biblical interpretation trying to explain which words Jesus actually said.[1] These scholars have spent little time discussing the effect of the sermon on the audience. The Gospel attributes all of these words to Jesus. The text is framed as a speech or discourse that covers approximately three chapters. This was not Jesus' only sermon, but Matthew's audience heard this message as a unit within the larger Gospel.

We can study the sermon as such—a message to an audience in the early years of the church. Without an audio recording of someone preaching Jesus' sermon, we need to immerse ourselves in the literary and cultural milieu of the Greco-Roman world to imagine what an audience expected to hear if someone preached Jesus' sermon to them. Matthew's church heard this portion of the text (and the rest of the book) read to them, and they responded to the Gospel. It is appropriate for us to read the text aloud to hear the nuances, to ask questions, and to gain a greater understanding of what Jesus said. When we listen to the sermon (or hear ourselves read it) with some awareness of the first-century Mediterranean culture, we gain new insight into who Jesus was, how he came to be viewed as an authoritative teacher, and the kind of power we receive through taking this message to mind and heart.

How to Read the Sermon on the Mount

Public recitations follow certain rules. Dr. Seuss's *Green Eggs and Ham* requires a different kind of nuance than a speech at the Rotary Club. Persuasive speeches in the first century followed rules as well. Sermons like the one in Matthew 5–7 were deliberative speeches that followed the patterns of ancient rhetoric outlined in the handbooks of Quintilian and Theon of Alexandria and practiced as far back as Aristotle through the Roman period to Cicero. Documents were read much like they were spoken. The reader/lector imitated the patterns of the speaker in the text, and the reader had the manuscript to guide him (Theon, *Progymnasmata* 115-116; Quintilian, *Inst.* 11.1.40). When someone recited a sermon, he tried to imitate the original speaker's mannerisms, vocal inflection, and tone. He created the impression that the original speaker was in the room. (Richard Ward calls this a rhetoric of "performance and presence" in "Pauline Voice and Presence as Strategic Communication," *Semeia* 65 [1994]: 101.) In the case of the Sermon on the Mount, the speaker imitated Jesus in such a way that the audience could imagine that Jesus himself was speaking the words to them. (For even greater detail, see my book *Reading Acts: The Lector and the Early Christian Audience* [Boston: E. J. Brill, 2004], 207.)

The first rule was "Know thy audience." Speakers adapted the content to the audience, and the crowd and speakers worked together as they would in the Greco-Roman theater or a modern African-American congregation in the South.

Speeches like the Sermon on the Mount were structured much like a persuasive speech today. They began with praise for the crowd of people around them (the proem or prologue), followed by the purpose of the speech, the instructions or topics for the listeners, and a conclusion with a closing challenge. Jesus' famous sermon does not fit neatly into any category, but it does have a recognizable structure (Talbert, *Reading the Sermon on the Mount*, 25).

Figures of speech were employed to demonstrate the meaning of the text. In the sermon, Jesus frequently used antithesis, a figure of speech from Greco-Roman and Jewish oration: "You have heard it said . . . but I say unto you . . . ." This was a common way to cite a maxim or commonly held saying that most in the audience understood. In this case, he quoted from the oral law or interpretations of the law that the people learned from religious teachers. Like a rabbi or philosopher, he added his interpretation and applied the teaching to his listeners. The assumption of the sermon was that, by listening and following the message, the believer, too, would be like the "wise man who built his house on rock" (7:24).

Phrases could be turned with jest, humor, and asides, and audiences could respond with "Amens," "Boos," and even applause. My assumption is that the breaks that seem unnatural were actually natural pauses in the text for an audience to respond. For instance in the Sermon on the Mount, Matthew 7:6 appears abruptly and has little connection to the statement on judging in 7:1-5 or the statements on prayer in 7:7-12. The line, however, may have evoked a reaction from the audience: "Do not give what is holy to dogs; and do not throw your pearls before swine, or they will trample them under foot and turn and maul you." We might assume that Jesus quoted a common saying from his day, then paused to invite the audience to agree.

A speaker also used humor to make his point. He imitated the habits, mannerisms, and quirks of characters in the culture, especially if he wanted to use them as a negative example. Much like a character in a play, stock figures were used to lighten the mood, evoke laughter from the audience, and drive home the point. The proud and arrogant were among the characters that speakers often imitated to evoke laughter from a crowd. Speakers who wanted to imitate others exaggerated their gestures, made strange faces, and spoke loudly, all for humorous effect. (Cicero discussed this technique in *De Oratore* 2.59.238 and employed it in his speech *Pro Cluentio*.)

In the sermon, the "scribes and the Pharisees" function as the stock characters. The Pharisees were laymen who thought non-priests should abide by the same Jewish purity laws that priests obeyed. Their scribes controlled the interpretations of Mosaic Law because they could read and write. Whether it is a fair characterization or not, the scribes and Pharisees had reputations for pride and arrogance. Their mannerisms and attire suggest that they acted superior to others. They practiced double tithing. For instance, in the parable of the publican and Pharisee (Luke 18:9-14), the Pharisee pays a tithe on his wages and his purchases. In Matthew 23, Jesus criticizes scribes and Pharisees. Their speech and actions did not match; they majored on minor things; they missed the message of Jesus; they looked for human praise; they persecuted messengers; and they tried to avoid the intent of the law (Talbert, *Reading the Sermon on the Mount*, 64).

Their clothes symbolized their dysfunction. In 23:5, the scribes and Pharisees "do all their deeds to be seen by men; they make the phylacteries broad and their fringes long, and they love the place of honor at feasts and the best seats in the synagogues."

These religious men placed scraps of manuscripts in boxes called phylacteries and strapped them to their foreheads and forearms. In their view, they were keeping the word of God close to the mouth and heart (Deut 30:14; see Figure 1).

The tassels were long strands on the sleeves and bottom of garments worn by religious teachers. According to Matthew, scribes and Pharisees wore extreme versions of these "fringes," making their appearance off-putting and intimidating. Because such a costume marked scribes and Pharisees distinctively (much like an actor wears a costume in the theater), the clothes provided fodder for anyone who imitated them. More importantly, their outward show kept them from addressing significant matters of the heart.

Figure 1.
Artist's concept of a Pharisee

Reading the Sermon on the Mount

THE SPEAKER (5:1; 7:28-29)

Thus far in these studies, we have learned that Jesus had a miraculous beginning from a family that transcended the normal cultural boundaries. Foreigners greeted and worshiped him. He was and is "God with us" (Matt 1:18).

Now, like a philosopher or rabbi, Jesus gathered with a circle of disciples (5:1) and taught them. The content of the sermon shows that he had authority greater than one of the popular philosophers or rabbis of the day (7:28-29; Talbert, *Reading the Sermon on the Mount,* 16).

THE AUDIENCE (5:1-12)

In the crowd were the disciples and a group not typically invited to a philosopher's or rabbi's lectures. Jesus blessed them, much like a contemporary speaker acknowledges the crowd.

Jesus noted that the crowd was qualified to enter the kingdom of heaven. As opposed to others whom people admired in their day (and in ours), the poor in spirit, mourners, meek, hungry and thirsty for righteousness, merciful, pure in heart, peacemakers, and persecuted fit the characteristics of a person who "hears these words and acts on them" (7:24-25).

Probably with a smile on his face and a look of encouragement, the speaker acknowledged the people in the crowd whom no one noticed. Because of their station in life as people ignored, overlooked, or abused, they were on the bottom of the religious ladder. Jesus blessed them, elevating them in the kingdom of heaven to the same level as everyone else.

In marked contrast, he parodied the "Pharisees and teachers of the law." The message takes common statements from the religious experts and, in a play on words, mimics their actions. The statements likely evoked smiles or laughter from the audience and allowed them not to be intimidated by those on the outside who appeared to be closer to God.

THE MESSAGE (5:13-7:27)

The sermon announces a simple message of obedience: the listeners met all the requirements needed to enter the kingdom of heaven, and these people were to be admired. Many in their society acclaimed the scribes and Pharisees, and they enjoyed the praise.

The sermon, however, portrays them as "hypocrites," the same word the Greeks and Romans used for "actors." They worried about outward appearances like actors on a stage rather than focusing on actions that shape a relationship with Jesus.

Just as comedy in the Greco-Roman theater employed stock characters to evoke humor, the image of the scribes and Pharisees is prevalent in the sermon. Jesus could imitate them easily, not only through nonverbal gestures but also by disarming the crowd and evoking laughter.

Following the prologue, the sermon announces the basic theme: that Jesus has not come to discard the law (5:17). He does, however, fulfill the basic intentions of the law by returning people to the matters of the heart. In jest, Jesus stated, "Unless your righteousness exceeds that of the scribes and Pharisees, you will never enter the kingdom of heaven" (5:20). The Pharisees' "righteousness" was no better than anyone else's. They could not get the basics right and were poor examples of obedience.

Their oral interpretations of the Jewish law demonstrate the degree to which they missed the point of the law. The sermon cites several examples in the antitheses (5:21-48). In the first part of each antithesis, Jesus quotes his opponents' interpretations and implies they have spread false information: "You have heard it said [by the scribes and Pharisees] . . . ." Their lives do not match a proper understanding of the law. Four examples are enough to make the case: they break the rules regarding anger (5:21-26), marriage (5:27-32); integrity (5:33-37); and retaliation (5:38-48). The intent of the law is to cause people to live with forgiveness, faithfulness, honesty, and love.

Scribes and Pharisees behaved more like actors than authentic, obedient believers. Session 6 lists several common features of these actors. They don a mask (or in this case, religious garb) and perform when they give, pray, and fast. They give their alms in such a way that others will applaud their actions. The giving receptacles in the temple and presumably in the synagogues were shaped like shophar trumpets. When the coins went into the chests, the money resonated and could be heard in the hall (see Figure 2).

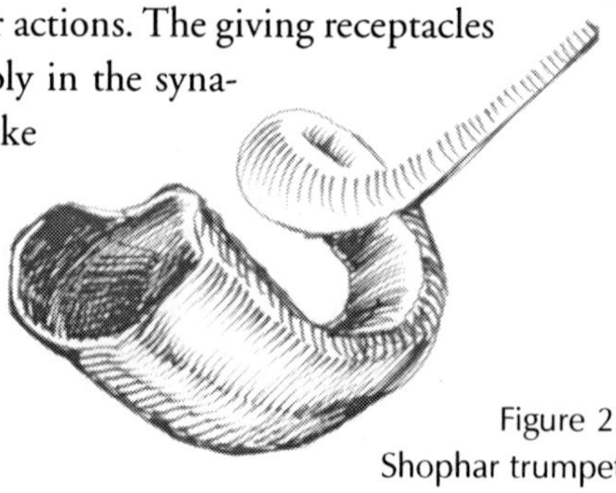

Figure 2.
Shophar trumpet

Their prayers were public spectacles as well. The common gesture of prayer in the first century—hands raised toward the sky—drew enough attention to the person. Pharisees and scribes took the practice one step farther and stood in the public squares praying so that others could see them (6:7-15). Fasting was also a public event for them (6:16-18), and their disfigured faces reminded people of the masks actors wore on the stage.

Jesus offers an alternative, and the model does not come from the Pharisees. His life was an example of his instructions. Behavior that shapes character is best performed privately. Giving is not based on the size of the gift. The giver should live so generously that giving is second nature (6:3-4).

We should handle prayer to God personally, realizing that the location and attitude of our prayers affect how we relate to God. Just as we converse with people individually at home, we can address God privately, away from centers of worship and out of sight of others (6:5-15). The language of prayer should reflect a desire to seek and obey God's desire for our lives. As A. J. Conyers was known for saying, "The Lord's prayer does not contain the phrase, 'Thy kingdom come; Thy will be done *in my life.*'" Prayer creates dependence on God for direction and yields to God's wishes. In that spirit of dependence, we ask things from the Father as a child requests things from loving parents (7:7-12).

Fasting is private and personal. This is the only New Testament passage that teaches people how to fast, and Jesus shows that fasting is a private act designed to cleanse the mind and body and make us more open to God. No one should be able to recognize that another person is fasting (6:16-18).

The words in the text indicate how we may read this section. Because Jesus mimics the actions of the Pharisees, we can imagine later speakers of his words using nonverbal gestures to parody the Pharisees, hands upraised to imitate their prayers, disfigured facial expressions to imitate the effects of fasting, and exaggerated gestures that evoked laughter.

The scribes and Pharisees missed the basics, and their mistakes are instructive. How can we work to imitate Jesus and follow his instructions (6:25–7:23)? The following list offers suggestions:

(1) Seek God first (6:25-34). Faithfulness to the first commandment—love the Lord your God with all your heart—helps us avoid

the anxieties that come with comparison and monetary challenges. Dependence on God results in rest and freedom from worry.

(2) Live authentically without comparison to others (7:1-12). The Pharisees and scribes judged others and ignored their own faults. By living authentically, believers understand that we all have faults.

(3) Let your behavior match your words (7:13-23). Actors live differently off stage, but believers' public deeds should match their private actions and words.

When we follow Jesus' instructions, we demonstrate that we have heard his message. Our lives are stabilized and strong enough to weather life's storms (7:24-27). The sermon (and subsequent recitations) shows Jesus' authority and empowers the meek, merciful, persecuted, and others addressed in the opening lines. Instead of feeling threatened or intimidated, they laugh, knowing that God does not compare them to other religious "experts." Their identity is rooted in their relationship to the one who loves them and communicates directly to them.

HEARING THE SERMON PREACHED

The sermon as an oral unit takes listeners back to the early years of Matthew's church as they heard it recited for the first time. Listeners can draw closer to that first-century audience and connect the ancient world to their modern one.

I have recited the Sermon on the Mount from memory four times in three different cities. In each case, I donned first-century garb and performed the text from memory in the style that I imagined it might be read. Three times, I performed the text individually; once I used assistants to pantomime various scenes. In each case, the effect was the same. The audience heard the Scripture in a fresh way. (Interestingly, it takes about 20 minutes to recite, or the average of length of one of my sermons.) People who normally read the text silently walked away with a new understanding. Hearing vocal inflection, jest, and laughter or seeing pantomimes caused people to understand the text differently. Hearing the sermon as a unit not only allows the listener to enjoy it from beginning to end but also reveals a new dimension to Jesus' personality in Matthew. He knew how to turn simple statements into clever phrases that disarmed opponents and enlivened a crowd. Matthew does not indicate that Jesus was a comedian, but we do come to see that Jesus had a good sense of humor.

Hearing the sermon preached, however, does not only benefit the listeners—the performer is affected as well. Each time I prepare to recite the text, I hear something new; I find fresh nuances in the text. I add an actor or two to the pantomime to demonstrate the activities in the text, and these changes alter my heart and mind. Anyone who prepares to recite a passage such as the Sermon on the Mount gains a new understanding of the text through the effort of committing the speech to heart, but he or she does not need to memorize the words verbatim to receive this benefit. Through researching the culture to find the nuances, paraphrasing the statements in his or her own words, and reading them among groups of people in order to listen for their interpretations, the speaker experiences the text in new ways.

In so doing, we hear the words and put them into practice, not as actors on a stage but as believers in the arena of life. No masks or costumes are required—simply an authentic believer imitating the one who, according to Matthew, had something to say to everyone and whose life matched his speech on and off the stage.

1. What is the greatest speech you have heard? What made it memorable? The speaker? The context? The events in your life at that time?

_____
_____
_____
_____
_____
_____

2. Read Matthew 5:29-30. These statements are hyperbole, intentional exaggeration used for effect. How can you read these aloud in an exaggerated tone representative of hyperbole?

_____
_____
_____
_____
_____
_____

3. Reading is interpreting. Studying the Bible requires not only comparing multiple versions of the same text but also multiple ways of reading the text aloud. How does reading the Sermon on the Mount aloud or listening to someone preach it change your interpretation of Jesus' image? How would hearing the text read aloud by multiple readers affect group study?

_____
_____
_____
_____
_____
_____

4. Imagine yourself in various locations to hear the sermon: in the crowd of those "blessed," in Matthew's church, and in a congregation of believers today. A person in the 1960s in Mississippi heard the text differently than someone in New York City in 2001. How should the context of the first century affect interpretation in another time and location?

_____
_____
_____
_____
_____
_____

5. Watch this scene from *The Visual Bible* DVD, Matthew 5–7: 26:36–36:36 (dir. Reghardt van den Bergh, GNN International, 1997). Notice how the editor portrays both Matthew's recitation of the text to the scribes and the character of Jesus preaching the Sermon on the Mount. Jesus laughs and interacts with the crowd. Do these moments complement the sermon or distract from it?

_____
_____
_____
_____
_____
_____

Note

[1] See, for example, James M. Robinson, *A New Quest of the Historical Jesus* (London: SCM Press, 1959); John Dominic Crossan, *The Historical Jesus: The Life of a Mediterranean Jewish Peasant* (New York: HarperCollins, 1993), 103-123; Robert W. Funk, *The Five Gospels: What Did Jesus Really Say?* (San Francisco: Harper Collins, 1997), 140.

Who Followed Jesus?

Matthew 8–12
Focal text—Matthew 8:28–9:36

The adage is right: "You can't judge a book by its cover." You can, however, assess a leader by the way he garners followers. Who is in the inner circle? Who follows? Who counsels? Who receives first priority? Jesus defied expectations when he reached out to the people listed in Matthew 8:28–9:36. Many people followed Jesus outside the circle of the Twelve. He used the power of a large network to draw others into relationship.

In this passage, Jesus encounters people whom members of the Jewish religious establishment classified as "sinners." They were each one of three types of people uninvited to worship in the temple: the mentally unstable, the physically disabled, and the politically criminal. Jesus' actions indicate, however, that everyone has a place in his kingdom, especially those disenfranchised by established religion.

Invitations to Follow

THE DEMON-POSSESSED (8:28-34)

After Jesus calms a storm for the first of two times in Matthew, he arrives in a God-forsaken cemetery in the Gentile region of the Gadarenes. Cemeteries were considered haunts for evil, and those tortured by the forces of darkness had only the tombs for protection. Greco-Roman cemeteries like this one, located outside the cities, often contained statues of family members, mosaics of loved ones, and trinkets of the dead. The monuments depicted physically what haunted the mind of demoniacs mentally.

In the first century, people classified as demon-possessed might have been afflicted by a whole range of modern-day illnesses involving the brain: Alzheimer's, epilepsy, autism, depression, or schizophrenia. In Jesus' day, they were banished from the city and were forced to live among the memories of loved ones.

In this case the demoniacs lived among the tombs, perhaps a reference to the grief that triggered their demons. Mentally disabled, these men could not speak for themselves; the demons shouted instead (8:29). They knew more about Jesus than the townspeople and addressed him as "Son of God." They represented the classic case of the forces of darkness identifying the divine man before others recognized him. Jesus faced the evil and spoke a word of healing that drove the forces of darkness into a herd of pigs. The townspeople responded in fear and asked him to leave (8:34). As David Garland noted, "They are more at home with the demons they know than with a power they cannot comprehend" (*Reading Matthew,* 102).

THE PARALYTIC (9:1-8)

In Matthew, Jesus first reaches out to the mentally disabled. Then he approaches the physically disabled, a paralytic. This encounter occurs in three parts. First, others inspire Jesus. Instead of Jesus' going to this individual, others in the community brought the paralytic to him. These people believed in the power of Christ enough to carry another person to Jesus. The phrase "When he saw their faith" (9:2) captures the moment. Something about their faith—not the faith of the paralytic—inspired Jesus.

The second step is spiritual healing. Jesus forgave the man, an act that incited the local religious teachers' ire. His spiritual language disturbed them, but their words betrayed the evil in their hearts. They accused him of blasphemy three times (9:3, 11, 14), a generic term in the culture describing anything associated with "acting in God's place" (Boring, "Matthew," 234). This is the first overt opposition to Jesus since his birth. The encounter that took place in Capernaum, "his home" (9:1), shows the larger concern of conflict with the religious leadership even outside Jerusalem.

In the third step, Jesus healed the paralytic physically after he healed him spiritually. The scribes learned that Jesus had authority to provide spiritual healing, and the crowds responded with awe and praise to God.

THE TAX COLLECTOR (9:9-17)

Others malign the third category of followers because of their crooked political reputation. The incident in these verses is associated with the namesake of the first Gospel, Matthew.

As a toll collector, Matthew was likely wealthy, a rising star in the Roman tax system. The tax office served as the launching pad for successful political careers in the Roman system. Tax collectors could move up if they were able to bribe their way to the top. Matthew worked from a "tax office," the equivalent of a modern toll booth. Tax offices were located at city gates, where the collectors could assess payments on goods that people bought, sold, or transported into a city. Depending on the agreement with the collector, a portion of the taxes was sent to the governing officials and to Caesar in Rome. Tax collectors kept an amount for themselves as their commission or earnings. These rates were set at the discretion of the individual collector and could be enforced by a local magistrate. Those who refused to pay were subject to arrest or further fines. As with everything in the Roman patronage system, some paid, and the wealthy could bribe their way out of payment. The system was subject to corruption, and tax collectors like Matthew developed terrible reputations that they probably deserved (Hanson and Oakman, *Palestine,* 115–16).

Jesus not only commanded Matthew to follow him (9:9), but he went to his house to share a meal, a sign of true friendship (9:10). The visit was also a threat to religious authorities.

When questioned about his actions, Jesus explained that what he did should be viewed as a wedding feast rather than a ritual ceremony (9:15). Just as people celebrated the groom when he was at the wedding, people celebrated God's presence in Jesus while he was present among the people. Echoing Isaiah, Amos, and Micah, Jesus said God wants mercy for people who have strayed. Believers demonstrate mercy by showing hospitality to sinners and people who have been left out of the religious customs.

THE CORPSE AND THE MENSTRUATING WOMAN (9:18-26)

Jewish law forbade men to touch a dead body or a menstruating woman. Both acts made a person unclean for worship in the temple. In this scene, a menstruating woman attempts to touch Jesus' clothes, and then Jesus touches a woman who was thought dead.

These characters provide examples of the risks Jesus took to reach out to those considered untouchable.

In 9:18, the leader of the synagogue implores Jesus to raise his daughter. As Jesus heads toward their house, an anonymous woman maneuvers through the crowd. This story, with one of the few references to Jesus' apparel, implies that he was wearing the traditional attire for Jewish religious teachers, complete with tassels that touched the ground (see figure 1). Without disturbing anyone, the woman touched the tassel.

Despite being rushed to the house of a prominent official, Jesus took time to acknowledge the woman's interruption. He turned, saw her, and told her that her faith made her well, implying a physical and spiritual healing.

When he arrived at the ruler's house, he dismissed the customary musicians and mourners who were paid to be at the scene of a funeral. He announced that the girl was still alive, and while those who heard him laughed, Jesus took the young woman by the hand and raised her back to life.

THE BLIND AND THE MUTE (9:27-34)

The last three examples of physically disabled individuals are three men—two who are blind and one who is mute. The blind men found Jesus in a house and were healed "according to their faith." Their first act of discipleship was an act of disobedience. Though Jesus warned them not to tell anyone about the healing, they spread the word anyway.

The mute man was also possessed by a demon, and Jesus healed him. The crowds, however, responded differently than the people in Gadara. These people marveled at Jesus' power, while the Pharisees attributed his work to the forces of darkness.

SUMMARY (9:35-38)

In the closing verses of chapter 9, Matthew summarizes his activities and sets the tone for the commissioning of the select group of twelve who lead the next mission. Jesus saw crowds struggling to endure the oppressive weight with no leadership. Compassionately, he prepared the disciples for a coming harvest in which they would participate.

For Jesus, seeking followers was a matter of finding people who had been classified as sinners and introducing them to a new kind of life. Some, like the people carrying the paralytic, the anonymous woman, or the blind men, demonstrated enough faith to be healed. Others, like the paralytic himself, the tax collector, or the demon-possessed, were simply welcomed because Jesus had compassion on them.

The way Jesus enlisted followers tells us who he is and what God is like. God seeks those whom most spiritual and secular people in society reject. Jesus was willing to risk his reputation to be associated with obvious sinners and people whom society considered incomplete because of their disabilities. He was willing to confront the opposition of religious leaders who falsely accused him.

The message that God's forgiveness is extended to all is an unnerving proposition. Each scene in these chapters follows the same basic pattern: forgiveness, objection, and Jesus' pronouncement (Boring, "Matthew," 235). The religious leaders rejected this formula. Their actions indicate that they were willing to hold on to retribution rather than risk liberation.

This message of forgiveness does not automatically mean, however, that a person will respond appropriately. Just as God gives humans freedom to choose to follow, so Jesus allows people to react freely. The text raises questions regarding the people's response. Why would the Gentiles of Gadara ask Jesus to leave (8:34)? What was the reaction by the healed demoniacs? Apparently, they did not follow Jesus. Did the paralytic want to be healed (9:2)?

Jesus also experienced the same problems in Galilean regions that he would experience later in Jerusalem. Some Gentiles did not welcome him with open arms, just as many Jewish people also rejected him.

Extending the Invitation Today

If this is the pattern of Jesus' invitations, his actions have negative and positive implications for the church. Negatively, the Calvinist notions of predetermined choices must be rejected. The Gospel witness is a call and response; both are significant to the relationship with Jesus.

Even Jesus struggled with recruiting followers. The mythical image that people automatically "left their nets" when they encountered Jesus' gravitas does not square with the stories in Matthew. Even those who needed the message did not always want the healing power of forgiveness.

Religious leaders especially struggled with the focus on forgiveness of sins. Blasphemy in this context seems to be the red herring used against an opponent. Jesus was willing to counter that with faithfulness to the people. Getting the message right can actually turn people away. The religious might accuse the believer of being "guilty by association" (a phrase suggested by Barbara Brown Taylor in her book *Home by Another Way* [Cambridge: Cowley Publications, 1999], 35). If we hang out with sinners, some will assume we have probably committed the same actions they have—or worse, we are possessed by the devil. According to this passage, a heart of compassion sustained Jesus, despite the opposition he faced, and attracted even more followers to his cause.

If Matthew 8–9 were used as a template for recruiting followers to Jesus, believers today should look for rather unlikely suspects to welcome into the kingdom. Unfortunately, church growth movements rarely target the mentally disabled, the physically deformed, the injured, or the known sinners for sharing his message. Most of the time, churches strategize about location, marketing, websites, and worship services.

Jesus offered a way forward that people can relate to today. He tried to find people others overlooked or cast out. He looked around for those who were "harassed and helpless," and most believers know the feeling of being left out and victimized. When we identify with the moments when we were the loner in the crowd, we understand a little more about the way Jesus invited people to discipleship.

In Matthew, Jesus welcomes everyone from the wealthy tax collector, upwardly mobile in a corrupt political system, and the socially outcast menstruating woman. Jesus does not fit neatly into the box of "focusing on the poor" or "targeting the outcasts." He seeks everyone and leaves the choices up to the individual.

Conclusion

When I first met Mary, she was already the mother of two children, one of whom was born before she married the father. She had long been classified as developmentally disabled. Because she did not own a car, she usually rode the bus to church with her parents or walked from her mother's nearby apartment. Occasionally a church member offered her a ride.

Mary's story could be replayed in a thousand different ways across the country. She was another person who dropped through the cracks of social services, and her family repeated a cycle of problems that were systemic for three generations.

Mary met her husband Frank in a life skills class at the adult high school. Both were mentally challenged; neither had the skills to parent, but both wanted to be parents in the worst kind of way. They married, and their issues with communication, finances, and other areas of life caused problems.

Mary had plenty of pride. She did not want a lot of help; she just wanted enough to get by, and she did not like handouts. The church assisted in every possible way. Several caring deacons and concerned church members rotated the transportation system, offered food and clothes when appropriate, took care of the children, and provided prescription medications. These were the immediate needs that were obvious on the surface and easily addressed by the church.

Frank and Mary were the kind of people whom Jesus likely encountered in his world. They were mentally disabled and underserved by a system designed to protect them. Through the love of caring believers, they were getting the support they needed.

Problems arose when Mary became pregnant again. As she was trained to do, the attending physician alerted Child Protective Services that the parents showed signs of being unable to handle three children. The older child was a rapidly maturing preteen, and the younger child was still in diapers and failing to thrive. The night they brought the third baby home, a social worker arrived to take the two babies away.

The system in the community did not have easy answers for this problem, nor did the Bible or the church. The church had been responsible to reach out to the family, so they felt it would be disingenuous to abandon them at this point. They also supported the role of the social service agencies because they could tell that the babies were not thriving as they should.

The incident began a long series of events, mostly hearings and custody battles with numerous problems. The family was frustrated because they had a long history of conflicts with government agencies and little reason to trust outsiders.

As the events unfolded, two things became clear: Mary and Frank were not qualified to be parents in the traditional American sense of the word, but they wanted to show love to the children as well as they could. The church also would not abandon the family. The members wanted to do everything they could to help Frank and Mary get their children back; more importantly, they wanted them to learn to become good parents.

At the same time, the social service agency contacted a group of nuns southeast of town. The group cared for children from difficult home situations. Through long negotiations with the family of origin, the court system found a way to allow the nuns to parent the children and the family of origin to have rights of visitation and maintain a relationship with the children. The nuns could provide the basic medical services the babies needed; the preteen could remain in the home; and the parents could have access to the children in a protected, safe environment.

The nuns and the church were not willing to give up on the people that society rejected. As followers of Jesus, they understood how to serve, heal, and attract more followers.

As the stories of Jesus' invitations, rejections, and pronouncements indicate, things rarely go as smoothly as planned. Even Jesus' summons to discipleship was greeted with skepticism, accusations, and rejection. Even today, stories of calling and following do not fit neatly in a box that can be shared on the doorstep of a home. People are invited into a relationship beyond the surface of appearances. When reading beyond the jacket cover of a book, we find that the stories become complex and often messy. This is true with people, especially those who might be mentally or physically challenged. The invitations and the responses only make the gospel an even better message for everyone.

1. With which people classified as "sinners" or outcasts could you be spending more time?

_____

_____

_____

_____

_____

_____

2. What are the difficulties in building relationships with the sick, the mentally disabled, or the poor?

_____

_____

_____

_____

_____

_____

3. When the HIV/AIDS crisis was first reported in the 1980s, some religious authorities announced that the disease was "God's punishment." Today, some of the same religious authorities encourage people to reach out to victims of HIV/AIDS, treating them with hearts of compassion. What made the difference? Is there a lesson to be learned in relating to other people classified as "sinners"?

_____

_____

_____

_____

_____

_____

4. What are the qualifications to be a follower of Jesus?

_____

_____

_____

_____

_____

_____

5. What are the implications of how society treats the mentally and physically disabled? If these are potential followers of Jesus, how should we treat them?

_____

_____

_____

_____

_____

6. Watch this scene from *The Visual Bible* DVD: 59:10–1:03:10. Notice how the editor uses the character of Matthew. He is present at the healing of the paralytic, becomes a follower of Jesus, and has Jesus as a visitor in his home following his call. In fact, the narrator supplies a word not in the NIV (or Greek version): Jesus goes to "Matthew's" house. How is the presentation also an interpretation?

_____

_____

_____

_____

_____

_____

What Did Jesus Do?

Matthew 13–20
Focal text—Matthew 14:13-33

Some of the greatest scenes in literature involve the sea. In ancient and contemporary writing, the sea supplies the backdrop for the founding of new cities or the emerging of new leaders. Recall just a few examples. Noah and the ark float to safety. Jonah flees his calling to be coughed up by a fish. Odysseus sails home as the hero to meet a son he has never known. Jason and the legendary Argonauts become the first humans to pass through the treacherous crashing rocks of Symplegades. Ahab encounters his nemesis in Moby Dick.

Worship in ancient Israel reflected this intimate connection with the sea and God's provision for life. The people saw the sea as the testing ground for their faith and a source of provision. They reflected on God's deliverance from the sea, God's provision of water, and God's further blessing of bread for their hunger. Psalm 78:13-25 is one of the few places that capture these images poetically (Garland, *Reading Matthew,* 155; note that the emphases are mine):

> He divided the *sea* and let them pass through it, and made the *waters* stand like a heap. In the daytime he led them with a cloud, and all night long with a fiery light. He split rocks open in the wilderness, and gave them drink abundantly as from the *deep.* He made *streams* come out of the rock, and caused *waters* to flow down like rivers. Yet they sinned still more against him, rebelling against the Most High in the desert. They tested God in their heart by demanding the food they craved. They spoke against God, saying, "Can God spread a table in the wilderness? Even though he struck the rock so that water gushed out and torrents overflowed, can he also give bread, or provide meat for his people?" Therefore, when the Lord heard, he was full of rage; a fire

was kindled against Jacob, his anger mounted against Israel, because they had no faith in God, and did not trust his saving power. Yet he commanded the skies above, and opened the doors of heaven; he rained down on them manna to eat, and gave them the grain of heaven. Mortals ate of the *bread* of angels; he sent them food in abundance.

The Sea of Galilee became the staging area for some of Jesus' greatest moments in Matthew. In the Gospel, the disciples journey to discover Jesus' identity and to imitate his life, emerging as a community of believers who worship him. They also receive nourishment from him as the bread of life.

To explain Jesus' deeds (and how we should imitate them), Matthew takes us by the sea. We have already learned a bit about Jesus' identity. We know his family history (Matt 1); his birth (1–2); a summary of his teachings (5–7); and a bit about his followers (8–12).

Jesus' ministry, however, does not always have the desired effect. Just as we saw in the previous sessions, despite his upbringing by faithful Jewish parents, the hometown crowd rejects him (12:46–13:58). Jesus himself feels the grief and pain of loss when his cousin John the Baptist is executed (14:1-12). In response to these events, Jesus attempts to get away but is mobbed by a crowd clamoring for more (14:13).

Imagine how Matthew's band of believers responded to these claims. These issues were just as significant for Matthew as he explained to a local church who Jesus was. They might have wondered, "If Jesus was rejected by his family, why should we follow him? What actions give us reason to believe in him? How can we know that he is not just another fly-by-night Messianic figure? If he wants us to imitate him, what exactly are we supposed to do?"

The writer of Matthew answers these questions with two miracles in this pivotal passage of the Gospel. The first miracle demonstrates publicly who Jesus is, and the second is a private explanation for the disciples.

Public and Private Miracles

THE FEEDING OF MORE THAN 5,000 (14:13-21)

The only miracle recorded in each Gospel is the feeding of more than 5,000 people. In this study, we have focused on passages unique to Matthew. This miracle is notable because of its popularity among the early Christian writers. Each Gospel uses the miracle to illustrate the themes of the book. Matthew's version occurs when Jesus arrives in a boat on the eastern shore of the Sea of Galilee. Now in Gentile territory, Jesus tried to take a break. The crowds noticed him, and he had compassion on them.

The disciples worried that they would not have enough resources to care for the people. They suggested that Jesus "send the crowds away" to fend for themselves (14:15). Jesus turned this into a teachable moment for the disciples: "They need not go away; you give them something to eat" (14:16).

Jesus' response was the heart of the issue: could the disciples learn to be responsible for problems once Jesus had withdrawn from them permanently? At first the answer was no because they saw only their limited resources, the five loaves and two fish. Jesus said the supplies given to him were enough to fill the people. He took the five loaves and two fish, gave thanks for them, and distributed the pieces. Everyone ate, and enough food remained to fill twelve baskets.

The events brought to the disciples' lives the same series of events from the historical memory of Israel. As Psalm 78 suggests, the Israelites struggled with bread. They complained and clamored when they were not fed.

The test for the disciples was slightly different. The Gentiles hungered much like the Israelites, but the resources were already provided. Jesus empowered them to utilize their common sense and faith in God. The disciples would soon be the leaders of the new Israel of God, the church. Jesus wondered whether they were ready to take the mantle of responsibility. God empowered them to feed the people just as God used Moses to feed the people in a lonely place in the wilderness. Matthew illustrates that Jesus provided bread for their hunger just as God provided manna in the wilderness, but the disciples failed to pass the test of leadership.

Even though the disciples failed, Jesus revealed another dimension of his identity. He is the king of the messianic banquet. Ancient adherents of Judaism believed that when the Messiah returned, he would host a great banquet or feast. These themes are evident throughout Jesus' parables and were mentioned as part of the wedding imagery in the previous lesson. When Jesus fed the Gentiles, he showed what kind of messianic kingdom he inaugurated. Unlike King Herod who feasted sumptuously, abused his power, lived immorally, and murdered Jesus' cousin (14:1-12), Jesus is a different kind of King. Herod was another incarnation of his wicked father, Herod the "Great" (2:1-12). Jesus offers a different kingdom. God provides enough resources; men, women, and children are fed (with leftovers to spare); and anyone can have access to the true righteous bread from heaven revealed in Jesus (Boring, "Matthew," 323; Parsons, "Commentary," 101).

The subsequent miracle echoes Psalm 78, again using water as the testing ground. In this scene, Jesus demonstrates his power over the waters and leads the disciples to safety (Garland, *Reading Matthew*, 155).

Jesus (and Peter) Walk on the Water (14:22-33)

Jesus' feeding of more than 5,000 people is arguably his most significant public miracle. The one that follows, his most significant private miracle, is viewed only by the disciples in a boat. The boat, mentioned once in the previous passage and five times in this passage, is the focus (Parsons, "Commentary," 106; emphasis is mine).

> [13] Now when Jesus heard this, he withdrew from there in a *boat* to a deserted place by himself.
> [22] Immediately he made the disciples get into the *boat* and go on ahead to the other side, while he dismissed the crowds.
> [24] but by this time the *boat*, battered by the waves, was far from the land, for the wind was against them.
> [29] He said, "Come." So Peter got out of the *boat*, started walking on the water, and came toward Jesus.
> [32] When they got into the *boat*, the wind ceased.
> [33] And those in the *boat* worshiped him, saying, "Truly you are the Son of God."

The disciples left the shore while Jesus departed from them. He prayed until around 3 A.M., the fourth watch of the night. The Romans called this time in the morning *intempesta* because of the frequency of storms. The waves tossed the small fishing vessel around, and the wind prevented the craft from sailing through the storm.

As Jesus walked out to join them (Mark's account says he "was about to pass them by"), the disciples were afraid and thought they saw an apparition. Their fears are understandable. These Jewish men grew up on the same stories others heard. The world was formed out of the sea (Gen 1:6); water caused death (Gen 7:4) and contained great fish (Jonah 1–2) and monsters (Job 41:1). They were caught in a storm, the ultimate sign of trouble; they were completely helpless and thought something could come out of the water to kill them.

Jesus responded with a word of assurance: "Take heart, it is I; have no fear." Uncertain that Jesus was who he claimed to be and unwilling to believe in the miraculous power in front of him, Peter looked past the evidence in search of feeling. He asked, much like the tempter in Matthew 4, "Lord, *if it is you,* tell me to come to you on the water." Jesus obliged his request, but Peter gave in to his boyhood fears and sank.

Unwilling to let the ambitious disciple drown, Jesus "grab[bed] him by the hand" and rescued him. When Jesus "[got] into the boat," the winds responded with calm. In turn the passengers worshiped him and acknowledged what they knew: "Truly you are the Son of God."

The Response of the Passengers

These two miracles reinforced a basic premise of life for the early believers. They could believe in Jesus because he is the Son of God. He demonstrated his relationship with God through miraculous power. He did not prove his power; instead, he used miracles to reveal his identity publicly and privately.

The disciples in the boat responded in two different ways. One responded by questioning the identity of Jesus, the others by worshiping. Could Peter be a model of faith to imitate or amusing comic relief in the midst of a dangerous storm?

At this point in Matthew, all we know about Peter is that he has left his nets (Matt 4) and has been listed with the inner circle of the Twelve (Matt 10). We know Peter will experience the transfiguration, a confession of Christ, Jesus' response, Gethsemane, and a denial firsthand. We know the end of the story, but Matthew has not revealed it yet. If we were reading this aloud to a group of people, we would have two events thus far, neither of which indicate that Peter was a leader.

Some say that in this passage, Peter models faith for believers. In John Ortberg's popular study *If You Want to Walk on Water, You've Got to Get out of the Boat,* the author offered the traditional interpretation of this passage. He said that, like Peter, we need greater faith; we need to take risks; believers should imitate Peter and do something new and challenging. "Getting out of the boat was Peter's great gift to Jesus; the experience of walking on water was Jesus' great gift to Peter" (Ortberg, *If You Want to Walk on Water*, 78).

Others, like Mikeal Parsons, say Peter's response is understandable but not commendable (Parsons, "Commentary," 108). The emphasis in the story, however, is not on Peter's reaction but on Jesus' power and the boat in which both sail. If we could walk on the water in our own power, as Ortberg says, we would not need a Savior.

In my view, the incident with Peter was likely welcome comic relief for a band of believers needing to see a new picture of Jesus and a realistic image of disciples. Sometimes Jesus' first followers moved ahead of him on the journey.

Jesus never asked Peter to get out of the boat; he responded to Peter's request. Peter initiated the activity, and Jesus gave him permission. Seeing Jesus walk and talk directly to them gave Peter enough evidence to believe in him. What more did he need? Jesus even asked, "You of little faith, why did you doubt?" (v. 31).

In these two miracles, Peter's response was to be that of the passengers in the boat: trust in Jesus as God and worship of him as the Son of God. They had already failed the test of leadership in the previous passage (14:16), not trusting God to make the most of the available resources. This time Peter's faith failed him again. He did not have sense enough to accept the evidence in front of him. The disciples needed to trust God for the journey whether they were out of bread in a crowd of 5,000, in an emergency, or sailing along for the ride. God did not require superhuman strength, just human trust.

The boat, a picture of the early church, reminded the passengers that they would encounter storms after Jesus withdrew (Matt 28:16). Just as Psalm 78 details the themes of God's provision (bread) and protection (water), so the story of the disciples' test with the bread and water reminded the early church how to imitate Jesus. Their best response was to trust in Jesus, work together, and worship him. He would be present in the midst of the storm.

They survived the storm by imitating Jesus and trusting him, not by attempting the spectacular. As they worked together, they became a new kind of faith family, a picture of what the early and modern church could be. They reached the other side and were leaders of an emerging community.

Sailing the Seas of Life

I have heard someone say, "If God wants to do something amazing, God starts working during a difficulty; if God wants to do something impossible, God starts working in a storm." We are asked to trust in a God who comes to us in the storm. Jesus' miracle shows us how to trust in the God of the storm even when we remain in the boat and work together.

When we experience storms as believers, sometimes we think God expects us to do something brave or risky. We forget that we have already accomplished the most courageous act yet. We trusted God, boarded the ship, and sailed. The anonymous writer of a familiar poem expresses this goal:

The Ship That Sails

I'd rather be the ship that sails
And rides the billows wild and free;
Than to be the ship that always fails
To leave its port and go to sea.

I'd rather feel the sting of strife,
Where gales are born and tempests roar;
Than settle down to useless life
And rot in dry dock on the shore.

I'd rather fight some mighty wave
With honor in supreme command;
And fill at last a well-earned grave,
Than die in ease upon the sand.

I'd rather drive where sea storms blow,
And be the ship that always failed
To make the ports where it would go,
Than be the ship that never sailed.
(http://www.storybin.com/builders/builders150.shtml [accessed 8 November 2007])

Paul Duke and Grady Nutt wrote the lyrics to a hymn that expresses the same themes:

We, O God, unite our voices, raised in thankful praise to Thee.
Thou, unchanging, safe hath brought us through the everchanging sea.

Days of calm and days of conflict, nights of darkness prove Thy grace.
Hands beneath us, arms around us, and, above, Thy shining face.

Seeing then the task before us bind our hearts and hands as one.
May our labor be in union, our resolve and Thine be one.
With one spirit let us labor toward the bright horizon far.
In the midst of tempest peril be Thy cross our guiding star.

Not our choice the wind's direction, unforeseen the calm or gale.
Thy great ocean swells before us, and our ship seems small and frail.
Fierce and gleaming is Thy myst'ry drawing us to shores unknown:
Plunge us on with hope and courage 'til Thy harbor is our home. ("We O God, Unite Our Voices," lyrics online at http://www.crescenthillbaptistchurch.org/oldsite/chhymn.htm [accessed 25 April 25 2007]).

When we make mistakes, such as leaving the boat unprompted, however, it is important to laugh at ourselves. There will be times when we attempt the impossible and learn again that God rescues us even when we look foolish. Learning to laugh and learning from our faults go hand in hand with faith. Just as Jesus laughed in Matthew 5–7 (see session 3), so we learn to laugh at ourselves through the lessons of Peter's life.

Learning to wait in the boat is not easy. It's much harder to worship, reflect, and work together with believers than to leave the boat of the church like a loose cannon. The old mantra, "If you want something done right, you might as well do it yourself," does not always hold water or keep us from sinking. Sometimes the best bet is to see God in the storm and keep sailing with the passengers.

This lesson is especially hard to learn in a culture where it's easier to church-hop than to remain in the boat to ride out a storm. Choosing a church community is not like shopping for a sailing vessel. We do not choose churches based on the programs or services they deliver. As Bonhoeffer says in *Life Together*, we receive the community as a gift and work together during difficulties (5).

Most clergy and lay leaders who have "abandoned ship" during difficulty will confess in hindsight that every church has pretty much the same problems. There are no perfect boats, organizations, or churches. When people leave over lack of programming for the kids, choice of worship styles, or problems with leadership, usually the solution is not found inside the safe confines of another church. It can be incredibly difficult to stay where we are and assist other passengers through the storm.

The passengers currently on board the boat cannot ignore constant maintenance of the ship either. Simply sailing along adrift at sea is not sufficient for vital, faithful ministry in the twenty-first century. We must cultivate relationships, welcome outsiders, empower people, and make changes throughout the journey to remain a vibrant vessel for God.

When we survive the storm, something wonderful occurs. We form or renew the community with whom we sailed. New leaders— even the impetuous ones—emerge having learned a lesson the hard way.

1. Compare Psalm 78 with Matthew 14:22-33. What are the similarities and differences between the Israelites' troubles with bread and water and the disciples' troubles with these elements?

_____

_____

_____

_____

_____

_____

2. Psalm 78 is a song of worship. How were the disciples able to worship after they crossed the Sea of Galilee?

_____

_____

_____

_____

_____

_____

What Did Jesus Do?

3. Water and bread go together in daily church life through baptism and Communion. The waters of baptism are reminiscent of the journey the disciples took from one side to another. The bread served at Communion reminds us of the banquet on the shores of Galilee. How can these two ordinances remind us of the protection and provision of God?

_____

_____

_____

_____

_____

_____

4. When hungry or worried during storms, churches need to trust God for the resources to provide the needed bread and rescue. What storms does your church face? Is this a time to worship together as the disciples did or take a risk by jumping out of the boat? Where is your church going on the journey?

_____

_____

_____

_____

_____

_____

5. When you have been through a storm, what lessons did you learn? When you have been together with a group of people, which new leaders emerged after the storm that you did not recognize before?

_____

_____

_____

_____

_____

_____

6. Think of a time when you jumped too far too quickly. What did you learn?

_____

_____

_____

_____

_____

_____

7. Watch this scene from *The Visual Bible* DVD: disc 1, 1:55:06–1:58:00. The character of Jesus laughs as he grabs Peter, an interpretation that complements this study. Is this a satisfactory explanation of the text? How did you imagine the scene? When have you felt God's parental laughter?

_____

_____

_____

_____

_____

_____

Part II

Surprise Ending: A Week in the Life of Jesus

The first part of Matthew answers the major questions of Jesus' life: birth, significant sayings and events, and followers. As the climax of the book indicates, these are important identity questions. The Gospel writer offers several answers that reveal a picture of Jesus as the Son of God. He is unlike other leaders. Visitors from foreign lands greet his origins from humble beginnings. He speaks to the lowliest of people as if they were the ones to be emulated. He rejects the traditional interpretations of Mosaic Law in exchange for character-shaping actions of the heart. He models an authenticity that strips away the façade of religiosity to reveal a relationship with the living Son of God. He reaches out to people who do not seem to respond positively to his invitation, and he embraces people who are the least likely to change. His most intimate disciples are the slowest to learn and listen, but even they are protected and preserved for greater service yet to come.

Matthew's audience heard this portrayal of Christ as both informational and inspirational. As they learned more about Jesus, they were inspired to imitate aspects of his life. They were to worship Jesus as the Son of God, to listen to and obey his interpretations of Jewish law, to reach out to people in their own families and culture whose reputations were suspect or who came from a different ethnic background, and to take responsibility even with meager resources.

In the second part of the study, we turn to the last week of Jesus' life and the resurrection faith that followed. The chronology slows down, and the questions are simple: How did he die, and what happened after he died? By looking at the last days as Matthew does, slowly and methodically, we gain an even greater understanding of the most significant figure in the history of the world.

Surprise in the Temple

Matthew 21:1-22
Focal text—Matthew 21:1-22

Matthew's biography of Jesus is unlike modern tales of heroes. He explains the story like a writer from the first century. He describes Jesus' heritage, birth, followers, teachings, and key events. One of the most significant components of an ancient biography is the description of the person's death. The manner in which a person dies reflects the degree to which people should respect, honor, and imitate the individual.

Twenty-five percent of Matthew's Gospel describes Jesus' last week of life and subsequent resurrection and farewell. Unlike other ancient descriptions of heroes who died predictably, Jesus' last week contains a number of remarkable twists and turns. These elements of surprise involve not only what happens to Jesus, but also how the story is told. Matthew reminds the reader that the gospel surprises us in moments of crisis.

On the first day of Jesus' last week, we encounter the surprising reactions of the crowd and the unexpected response of Jesus to the temple system. In Matthew 21, Jesus exposes the corruption of the temple complex and demonstrates where God's presence can be found when the temple is gone.

The Institution of the Temple

The pilgrimage to sacrifice at the Jerusalem temple was the one great act of devotion carried out by faithful Jewish believers. Everyone assumed that the presence of God was within these walls. In practice, however, the temple became a symbol of the corruption when government and religion work together.

After Herod the Great conquered his opposition in the Galilean and Judean regions and secured his place as king, he began massive public works projects to curry the favor of the people and to provide a lasting legacy of his power. To gain favor with the religious leaders in Palestine, he gave the Jewish establishment what they always wanted, a temple building to rival Solomon's and to remind them of the days when the Israelite nation was united. Of course the temple had important religious functions. The place provided a centralized location for sacrifice; a common building united the people; and the priests carried out their duties (as best as they understood them) prescribed in the Hebrew Scripture (Hanson and Oakman, *Palestine in the Time of Jesus*, 76).

Herod's project was a masterful mixture of politics and faith; and his son, Herod Antipas, continued the construction. The temple reaped significant economic benefits for the Judean economy. Some Jews, if they were financially able, made four trips to Jerusalem to celebrate the religious festivals. Their presence meant money, tourism, and trade for the religious center.

The Passover festival was particularly beneficial not only because of its central significance in the Jewish year but also because it lasted a week. Guests and relatives filled homes and overflowed marketplaces, and the temple offices benefited tremendously.

The temple complex was more than just one building for worship. It was large enough to hold offices for staff, housing for priests, a slaughterhouse for sacrificing the animals, a plumbing system for the blood of the animals, a barn for livestock, and practice facilities for musicians (see Figure 3).

The staff of the temple numbered into the hundreds. There were the normal duties of burning animals and praying to God. Many other functions were significant in assisting the people to fulfill their obligations to God. Staff maintained order and discipline through the temple police officers, cared for the livestock, played music, cleaned the temple area, received offerings for sin, distributed money to the needy, allocated offerings to Herod and the Roman government, handled payroll for the Jewish leadership, and sold livestock to pilgrims coming for festivals (Hanson and Oakman, *Palestine in the Time of Jesus*, 140–41, 145).

Since most people did not have the ability or technology to transport the proper animals for sacrifice (or the means to keep them alive in transport), the temple staff provided a way for people to purchase the correct gift according to God's law. The poor were allowed to offer two turtledoves; others were required to offer

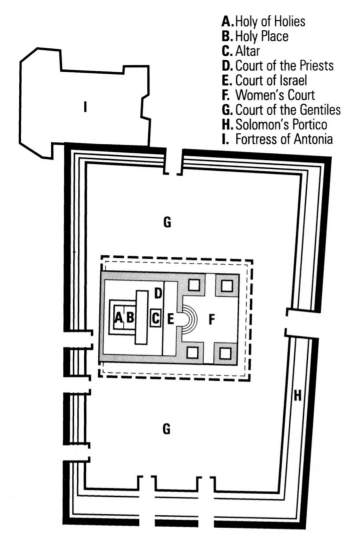

A. Holy of Holies
B. Holy Place
C. Altar
D. Court of the Priests
E. Court of Israel
F. Women's Court
G. Court of the Gentiles
H. Solomon's Portico
I. Fortress of Antonia

Figure 3. The Temple in Jesus' Day

pigeons. The animals were available outside the main temple building in the Court of the Gentiles.

This combination of economics, piety, and administration created a climate of dependence on the institution. The Jewish leaders saw the temple not only as the location of God's presence but also the place that provided for them financially and economically. The institution created a miniature system of power and control over the lives of the people in Judea.

As Matthew describes Jesus' first visit to the temple, each activity has theological significance. Like a faithful Jewish person, he arrived at the temple to fulfill his religious duty, making the pilgrimage with others and being greeted as a conquering hero. As he visited the temple complex, he showed the people what kind of king he was, exposed the corruption in this economic system, and replaced the institution as the presence of God for the people.

Jesus' Response to the Institution

THE HUMBLE KING (21:1-11)

On the top of the Mount of Olives, Jesus sent two unnamed disciples to the little nearby village of Bethphage to get a donkey and its colt. Two animals may seem odd to us, but it would not have been strange to Matthew's audience. Jesus' actions fulfilled the expectations of Isaiah (62:11) and Zechariah (9:9) to show people what kind of person he was. He was not a militaristic Son of David, like King Solomon, conquering people through bloodshed. He was the king who conquered through humility (v. 5). Two kinds of people greeted Jesus, the crowds outside the city and the people inside the city. One group was eager to hail a hero, and the other was disturbed by the reaction.

Jesus mounted the colt or donkey and rode into a welcoming crowd singing the familiar words of Psalm 118. Throughout Matthew's biography of Jesus, crowds like this repeatedly hailed him as "Son of David." They were the kind of people one would expect to see with Jesus. They had also heard the claims that Jesus was like Solomon, David's son, and would unify the country. The following examples from Jesus' portrait in Matthew added to his reputation among the crowd.

- Two blind men cried out for mercy to the Son of David. When they came into the house where Jesus was, he healed them (9:26-28).
- People heard the news that Jesus healed a demon-possessed man who was blind and mute, and in that moment they asked if he was the Son of David (10:23).
- Even Gentiles in the throng knew of the Gentile Canaanite woman who insisted that the Son of David heal her daughter (15:22).

Possibly remembering events like these, the people in the crowd just outside Jerusalem understood the importance of the moment. Jesus could heal, unify, perform exorcisms, and travel into Gentile regions unharmed. They cut palm branches and spread garments for him and announced to everyone, "Hosanna to the Son of David" (21:9).

By contrast, the people "in the city" of Jerusalem were "shaken" (v. 10). By implication in Matthew, they had not been with Jesus; they had not seen evidence of his power or heard his teaching. They had been tied to the institution of the temple and were disturbed by the possibility that someone of his stature could enter the city. They wondered who could cause such crowds to shout a title like "Son of David" and welcome someone during the Passover season with such adulation. They asked the significant question in the Gospel: "Who is this?" (21:10).

For the moment, the crowds outside answered the question: "This is the prophet Jesus from Nazareth of Galilee" (v. 11). They knew more about Jesus than the people in the city. They had followed him this far and were willing to continue. They had no idea what was about to happen.

The Corrupt Temple System (21:12-13, 18-21)

As the crowds spread the word about their hero, Jesus moved toward the temple complex, where he immediately confronted the institution in the Court of the Gentiles. He did not enter the rooms reserved only for priests but remained on the outside where everyone was welcome. There he observed two interesting scenes.

On the one hand, people spent money to fulfill their obligation to God (v. 12). On the other, the blind, lame, and outcasts in society—the kind of people who just greeted him outside the city—could not go any farther than the Court of the Gentiles and were rejected by the system. The implication is that with a temple system so large and vast, surely there would be a place for the indigent and infirm!

Outraged, Jesus turned over the tables to keep people from wasting their money any longer. He did not close down the slaughterhouse but disrupted the crowds, causing a disturbance that drew the people's attention. The corrupt temple system overlooked the people they were ostensibly serving. A portion of the offerings would have indeed gone to the blind and lame, but the combination of their presence in the Court of the Gentiles, coupled with the corruption of the religious leadership and Roman officials, made the place feel more like a "den of thieves" than a space to worship God. Jesus demonstrated that the temple failed in its mission (Garland, *Reading Matthew*, 211).

The system was more like a withering fig tree than a place of life and vitality. Even though on the outside it brought economic prosperity and visitors to Jerusalem, it produced no fruit in the lives of people. The place stifled faith instead of bringing life. Jesus illustrated the point the next day to the disciples (vv. 18-21). When he saw a fig tree with no leaves, he used it as an object lesson and demonstrated the problem with the temple. By forcing people to fulfill religious obligation while overlooking the poorest of the poor, they suppressed faith. In Jesus' view, the disciples could accomplish more without a building by using faith and prayer. They did not need a building, titles, or honors if they had a relationship with God.

THE LOCATION OF GOD'S PRESENCE (21:14-17)

To reinforce the point, Jesus welcomed the people the temple did not. He turned to the ones on the fringe of religion, treated the blind and lame as people, and embraced the children in the crowd.

By engaging them personally, Jesus demonstrated that God's presence was located in him—not in a structure. He began a new era of authority with them. When confronted by the temple staff who were indignant at his words, Jesus quoted their Scriptures to them. From now on, the people could come directly to him to gain access to God (Garland, *Reading Matthew*, 211).

THE INSTITUTION OF THE CHURCH

Ironically the people in the crowd knew more about God's presence in Jesus than those who were fulfilling the requirements of the law. By the time the crowds were absorbed into the temple, they gave in to the same foregone conclusion: Jesus needed to be eliminated so the temple could continue. In just a few chapters, even the crowds who once hailed him as Son of David cry out "Crucify."

Early believers read and understood Matthew's biography as instruction and warning: The effectiveness of religious institutions is measured not only by how many people they welcome but by the people they turn away. The church of today is only successful to the degree that it welcomes both the people who can jump through the hoops of membership, finances, friendships, families, Bible study, and worship *and* the people who are lost in the crowd.

Churches should not only to listen to the leaders who serve them but to the crowds who look and ask for a Savior but have been turned away by the institutional church. They point the way when the church asks, "How did Jesus live? What did Jesus do? What would he want us to do?"

One group crying out today is students and young people in their twenties. Christian denominations across America lament the loss of this demographic. Roland Martinson, in a recent study of Lutheran trends, wrote that "75% of young men and women leave the church between ages 16–24, and 40% who leave return by age 35; 30% of those who return go to other denominations" (Martinson, "Spiritual but Not Religious," 326). Students who grew up in their congregations exit through the door of graduation never to return. Research from interviews indicates that the trend has little to do with worship style and programs. Many of these young people as adolescents were able to attend worship services and/or religious programming that was tailor-made to their preferences and stages of life.

The exit trend has more to do with providing a place to ask questions without retribution from religious leaders. Martinson stated that one of the factors in students' decisions to return to church was whether they felt the church they attended as adolescents provided a safe place to ask tough questions and a place where they knew they could come "home."

Could the voices of young people be crying out in the crowd, asking for a place to learn more about the Savior? A quick glance at religious headlines reveals why the institutional church has lost its way with young people. If the lessons of the scandals caused in the Catholic and Evangelical churches, as well as the ongoing division within mainline Protestant and Baptist churches, are any indication, institutional churches have not had the emotional energy or remained secure enough in their relationships with Jesus to provide this place for students and young people. Believers must return to their role, pointing people to a relationship with Jesus Christ.

1. Jesus wasn't a new Solomon as Son of David; he was a spiritual Son of David. What's the difference?

_____

_____

_____

_____

_____

_____

2. Why did the crowds outside the city eventually give in to the religious leaders' accusations about Jesus?

_____

_____

_____

_____

_____

_____

3. Try to act out the passage. Assign these roles: members of the crowd outside the city, narrator, people of the city. Where do you see yourself? In the crowd? In the city?

_____

_____

_____

_____

_____

_____

4. Do you know anyone who attended your church but no longer attends any church? What can you learn from their experiences?

_____

_____

_____

_____

_____

_____

5. Churches seldom vote to keep people outside. The temptation comes more subtly through a simple nonverbal expression on a face, a prejudicial remark, or a missed opportunity. Even when the church is doing many good things, it can miss the most important things. What makes the difference between Jesus' response and the religious leadership's response?

_____

_____

_____

_____

_____

_____

6. Watch this scene from The Gospel according to St. Matthew DVD: 48:23–50:23. Discuss the contrast between the crowds inside and outside the temple courtyard. Notice the reactions of the children who enter the courtyard after the tables are overturned.

_____

_____

_____

_____

_____

_____

Predictions of a
Surprise Return (Parables)

Matthew 21:23–25:46
Focal texts—Matthew 22:1-14; 25:1-13, 31-46

As if Jesus' desire to upset the temple establishment was not enough, imagine the effect on the people when he shared his view of the future. Jesus' eschatology, his perspective on the end of time and the beginning of eternity, stirred controversy. Through a series of parables, Jesus explained that he would return when least expected and would judge the righteous and unrighteous.

Demonstrating Authority with Parables

On Monday of the last week of his life, Jesus returned to the scene of his table-turning incident. This time, instead of disturbing the people with a symbolic act, he taught them. This section of Matthew, the longest teaching passage in the Gospel, answers the religious leaders' question that they raise in 21:23: "By what authority are you doing these things, and who gave you this authority?"

Jesus answers as he has done before in Matthew with authoritative speech-acts called parables. In the Gospels, parables are the stories, comparisons, and analogies that help explain the kingdom of heaven and describe a reality beyond this world. Retelling parables or fables and drawing a conclusion from them were significant parts of rhetorical training for rabbis. When Jesus used parables, he demonstrated his authority, set the stage for the significance of his death and resurrection, and warned the people about his return as authoritative judge.

The Synoptic Gospels record about seventy-five of Jesus' parables. Matthew contains more parables than either Mark or Luke. Some, like the "Sower and the Seed" (Matt 13), were allegorical in meaning; others, like the "Lost Sheep" (Matt 18:10-14), encouraged an ethical response not to despise a "little one." Three parables in

Matthew 22–25 discuss the surprising nature of the kingdom of heaven.

Telling Parables of Surprise

THE WEDDING BANQUET: SURPRISE REJECTION (22:1-14)

What if your son or daughter were getting married, and no one wanted to come? What if you sent out invitations to the rehearsal dinner, and no one sent an RSVP? What would happen?

In Matthew 22:1-14, Jesus describes these conditions in the parable of the wedding banquet. He relates the kingdom of God to an allegorical depiction of a wedding banquet for which a king sends out customary invitations. In a culture where most people did not read, few formal written invitations were sent. Instead, a band of servants usually scattered to invite people to the "party of the century." A party thrown by a king would be outstanding.

According to some Jewish traditions, the wedding feast lasted a full week or two. Guests planned to stay for a while. In Jesus' parable, since the wedding is for the king's son, not everyone is invited to the festivities; but those who are invited receive royal treatment.

The first invitation prepares people for the arrangements (22:1-3). This formal announcement gave people time to make plans. A second invitation followed soon thereafter so people could know when the festivities began. With no refrigeration, people needed to drop everything at once to enjoy the slaughtered bull, sheep, and other delicacies (Scott, *Hear then the Parable*, 169).

When the servants arrive for the customary second invitation, the response is naturally surprising (22:4). People have had time to clear their schedules, but they still give excuses. Another group follows to issue more invitations. Their listeners give all sorts of excuses why they refuse to come, and they kill the servants.

Everyone listening to Jesus' story knew who he was talking about. He was describing the reaction of Jewish leaders to himself. God sent out invitations to the banquet. People refused to come, offering various excuses, and then they killed off the messengers—the prophets—thinking that would prevent people from coming to the party.

In the parable, the people's reaction makes the king more eager to invite others to the banquet. To paraphrase, he says, "If I cannot get the wealthy and the connected to come to my party, I will just make sure someone shows up." He sends more messengers to the poor sections of the country and says, "We have a seat for you."

Jesus explained that God involves people in his kingdom in a similar way. Using the same imagery employed when he forgave sins (9:15), Jesus said the kingdom is like a wedding for God's Son. God has invited people to join him at the wedding feast of his Son Jesus Christ. Who would refuse an invitation like that? Surprisingly, the first ones invited did. God sent his servants to ask even more to come. By implication, Jewish people were the first two groups to receive invitations and Gentiles the third. Another surprise awaited. Jesus indicated that accepting an invitation, knowing the groom as a "friend" (22:12-13), and attending the wedding are not enough. One must be clothed correctly, or prepared through one's obedient living, in order to enter the feast (Garland, *Reading Matthew*, 225).

THE BRIDESMAIDS: PREPARED FOR A LONG WAIT (25:1-13)

The following is my paraphrase of Jesus' parable about the bridesmaids:

Once upon a time people were awaiting the arrival of their hero, the groom. They were part of a wedding party, but for whatever reason, the bride was late. Maybe she needed to put on makeup, or the grandmother was delayed exiting the flight, or the groom left the rings back at the hotel. Things were running behind.

The wedding party did their part—they were at the church, waiting. Five of them, however, never expected it to take this long. They only brought one change of clothes and no extra food. They were tired and thought they would be home by now. After they had waited such a long time, all the bridesmaids finally fell asleep.

When the groom arrived, half of them were ready. They had oil in their lamps, and when they trimmed their wicks, the flame continued to burn to light their way to the feast.

The others were in town purchasing oil to refill their lamps. When they returned, they found that their companions had already joined the party. When the unprepared bridesmaids tried to enter the festivities, the groom turned them away at the door and acted as if he never knew them.

The lamp Jesus described was not a torch, a menorah, or even a candlestick, but more like a jar with a spout. Inside the spout was a wick that burned with proper trimming for about four or five hours. In Jesus' parable, the bridesmaids need the lamp to be prepared; they need the oil to burn brightly for the groom. Only five of them have a sufficient supply.

The groom arrives and finds half of them unprepared. He does not want to keep the bride waiting any longer. He enters the feast and shuts out the rest of the party. No one else can come in. By the time the rest of the wedding party arrives, the groom feigns ignorance. He acts like he does not even know them, and they are left out of the feast for eternity.

Some of Jesus' parables are difficult to decode. The characters in this parable initially sound familiar: a bridegroom and virgins/bridesmaids. But the story uses elements disconnected from reality. First, the bride is absent. Thus, the story is not about the bride's behavior or the features of the wedding.

Second, people in Jesus' culture shared resources. That the bridesmaids are unwilling to share the oil seems selfish. Most people would have willingly given their oil to another person whose lamp went out. We know this is not a story describing a life of generosity (Garland, *Reading Matthew,* 240).

Third, it was rare for a groom to be delayed; he was usually punctual. The parable is likely not about the timing of the groom.

It appears that this parable is about the preparation of the wedding party through obedience. Because they do not know when the groom will return, the bridesmaids must bring enough oil to endure his delay. According to the parable, two things cause the bridesmaids to be unprepared. The first is incorrectly predicting the groom's return. They focus on the time of the return and assume he will arrive when expected. The second is similar to the first: fixating on a sooner (rather than delayed) return. Both aspects cause them to deplete their resources.

The lesson is that those who expect Jesus' return or assume his coming will be quick will be sorely disappointed. No one knows when it will happen, and his return will never occur when expected.

The only thing a faithful person can do is to "keep watch," or live an obedient life whether awake or asleep. All the bridesmaids fall asleep, even those who are alert. The issue is one of preparation. The foolish ones think they know when he will return. Jesus indicates that obedient attendants are prepared for a lengthy wait (Boring, "Matthew," 451).

THE LAST JUDGMENT: NATURALLY SURPRISED (25:31-46)

The third parable, like the others, contains an unexpected twist. Instead of an issue of rejection or timing, this one involves reaction to the master's judgment.

A king separates good from bad much like a shepherd separates sheep from goats. These images were familiar in the Greco-Roman world. Jewish practices allowed sheep and goats to graze together, but Greco-Roman flocks were different. Because of the cooler climate outside Palestine, shorthaired goats needed shelter more often than wooly sheep. Shepherds separated the herds (Theocritus, *Id.* 1.80; Aelius Donatus, *Vit. Verg.* 49).

Greco-Roman culture also associated goats negatively with sexual promiscuity (Theocritus, *Id.* 5.147-50). When the king separated individuals according to behavior, the disobedient people were labeled as "goats."

The practices described in the parable seemed normal outside of Galilee and Judea. Jesus says the people considered "sheep" serve in ways such as taking in prisoners, putting clothes on babies, and giving drinks to thirsty individuals. The "goats" reject those who are needy.

The sheep and goats share one thing in common, however. Both groups are surprised—even dumbfounded—when the shepherd explains the reason for separation (Boring, "Matthew," 451). They say, "Lord, when was it that we saw you hungry and gave you something to eat?" (25:37, 44). In both cases, neither group knows that they are doing anything good or bad; they simply do what comes naturally to them.

Surprised by the Parables Today

REHEARSING THE WEDDING

The customs of an ancient wedding banquet are analogous to the modern wedding rehearsal and dinner. Even though our weddings do not last for a week, we rehearse the parts, prepare for the event, and feast together the night before the big day. In a rehearsal, the coordinator positions the attendants, practices the processional, and coordinates the instrumentalists. As the rehearsal goes, often so does the wedding itself.

In the same way, believers prepare for the wedding of Christ to the church each time we gather for worship and serve others. The bridegroom (Christ) has invited all people to come to his celebration. The guest list is open-ended; he has sent people to invite everyone because most of the first invitees refused to come.

When we gather in a church, the service functions like the wedding rehearsal. When we worship, serve, and study, we are learning our parts. We learn how to be obedient. We learn more about the groom and discover the others in the wedding party. We meet the other members of the family who are also on the bride's side. We study the groom's story (the Bible). We serve in other ways, too. We visit people in nursing homes, homeless shelters, hospitals, and prisons who wish they could attend the rehearsal.

The problem, however, is that most people are too busy to come for the rehearsal. They are busy getting ready for other things. They are either at the office working extra time on Sunday morning, going to the ball game, golfing another eighteen holes, or simply staying at home. In essence, many refuse the invitation. This is their choice. And it is none of our business to worry about their choices. Most of their decisions come naturally to them, and they would not think otherwise.

God says that in order to come to the wedding, though, we must accept the invitation and be prepared when we arrive. According to the parable, some "friends" who attend the rehearsal will not be at the wedding, just as there are plenty at church who are not fully prepared for the end.

To be prepared, we need the right garments. The clothes are not a description of the required attire for a worship service. They are the symbols of obedience. Righteousness is clothing for the feast. It is not enough merely to accept the invitation; we must live appropriately as well.

PREPARING FOR THE BRIDEGROOM

The preparation of the wedding party continues in the second parable. The parable reflects a common issue. Believers acknowledge by faith that Christ will return. No one knows when it will happen.

We are like the bridesmaids in the story, and he is our groom. We are part of the wedding party awaiting his arrival. We know he is coming, and all of us have lives (lamps) that we are leading. While awaiting his arrival, we do things that people normally do. We fall asleep, we go back to our jobs, we work in the community, we go to the soccer field and the youth retreat, we sing in the choir and wash the clothes. We rest and take Sabbath because that is what we are supposed to do.

While we are living life, Jesus says we prepare for the bridegroom's arrival. We prepare by having enough oil, or in our case, doing the things the groom told us to do. These responsibilities are listed in Matthew 5–7 in Jesus' Sermon on the Mount.

Unfortunately, many of us will not be ready because some make the same error as the foolish bridesmaids. Some of them thought they were supposed to predict when the bridegroom would come; they thought he would come sooner. They looked at the heavens, read a few books on the end of time, bought all the Christian novels about the beast and 666 they could find, and decided that surely *this* was the end of the world.

Jesus reminds us that a life focused solely on the time of the ending—or even maddening discussions disguised as the ending—misses the point altogether. He does not ask us to live with a heavenly time clock. In fact, if we do, those issues drain us of our oil. We can get so worked up about predicting the end that we forget about living the gospel in our lives today.

We remain alert through preparation, not by lying awake at night in a panic. The reason we lie awake is because we are worried that somehow we have not secured the place or have not fully prepared for a test. We go to sleep when we are prepared and when we trust that the groom will come on his schedule.

Changing What Comes Naturally

The third parable focuses on the significance of the ordinary decisions of life. The only thing sheep do well is what comes naturally—the things they have been trained and conditioned to do—and they do them repeatedly.

At the last judgment people will not be rewarded or condemned for the things they can remember doing; they will be judged on acts they did not notice, on the things that came naturally.

The most important question for our lives is not "What would Jesus do?" More critical evaluation is required. We must look into our hearts and schedules and ask, "Whom do I ignore when I am not even thinking about it? Whom do I miss because it comes naturally for me to rush by? Who never gets the cup of cold water because my calendar says it's time for a meeting? Who doesn't get the invitation to dinner because I am not sure if it would be safe to do something like that?"

The power of the cross and the resurrection changes even what comes naturally. If there is any power in Christ's work, he changes the way we think about what we do and the way we do things. He has the power to take our lives, our recordkeeping selves, and change them into the kind of sheep who take in his brothers and sisters and say to him, "Lord, we had no idea we were doing that, but thank you, O God, for giving us your kind of deliverance, your kind of suffering, your kind of love, your kind of shepherding."

1. Why did Jesus use parables to explain the kingdom of heaven?

_____
_____
_____
_____
_____
_____

2. How did these parables explain Jesus' authority?

_____
_____
_____
_____
_____
_____

3. How do these parables surprise you?

_____
_____
_____
_____
_____
_____

4. How can you be better prepared for the wedding of Christ to the church?

_____
_____
_____
_____
_____
_____

5. How do predictions of the return of Christ drain the "oil" from life?

_____
_____
_____
_____
_____
_____

6. Habits affect the heart. The more we do for others, the more naturally we respond to people in need. What kinds of activities should come naturally to believers?

_____
_____
_____
_____
_____
_____

7. Watch this scene from The Visual Bible DVD: disc 2, 55:17–58:19. Notice the character of Jesus' emotion in the closing verses. How do the listeners react? How would you?

_____
_____
_____
_____
_____
_____

Enemies Plot to Kill Jesus

Matthew 26:1–27:10
Focal text—Matthew 26:1–27:10

Dick Wolf's *Law and Order* programs have been a staple on NBC. In longevity, the original series is second only to *Gunsmoke*. What gives the show its distinctive quality is the unexpected twist. Between arrest, trial, and conviction, something happens to the suspect or the attorneys that changes the outcome. The events take place behind the scenes, always hidden from the viewer until the trial, when everything comes together.

When reading an ancient biography, we typically know the end of the story; the characters, of course, do not. In this section of Matthew, we read of Jesus' final encounter with the Jewish and Roman representatives of *Law and Order*. We meet the characters who play such fascinating parts and read how Jesus' trial takes an unexpected twist. Under the cloak of darkness, the religious authorities successfully plot to arrest Jesus, but they become unwitting accomplices in their own downfall.

The Major Characters

THE UNWITTING AUTHORITIES (26:1-5; 27:6-10)

This section of Matthew opens and closes in the house of Caiaphas the high priest. Valerius Gratus, a Roman procurator over Judea and Samaria, appointed him. Caiaphas served eighteen years as supervisor of the temple police and chief administrator of religious ceremonies. He remained in office when Pilate ascended to power. We know little about him as an individual, but his staying power in office is notable. After his brother Annas, whom Valerius Gratus fired, four other high priests were appointed in one year. Caiaphas, the fourth one, apparently possessed something that no one else had, an ear to the moods of the people (26:5) and the government (27:2). As the political and religious leader of the region, he influenced and enforced legislation. He convened a secret tribunal to deal with Jesus in violation of the Jewish code of the Passover (Brown, *Death of the Messiah*, 1:410).

THE UNKNOWN WOMAN (26:6)

The only person other than Jesus who understood the events was an unknown, unnamed woman. She appears briefly in 26:6-13 to anoint Jesus' body, preparing it for burial. The disciples missed the point and called her act wasteful. Jesus responded by saying her deed would be etched in the annals of history.

THE TRAITORS (26:14; 26:33)

Two members of Jesus' inner circle performed treacherous acts. Judas Iscariot, the betrayer of Jesus, appeared under the cloak of darkness as the agent of Caiaphas's tribunal. He exchanged the location of Jesus' prayer for thirty pieces of silver, fulfilling a prophecy from Zechariah 11:12 (Matt 26:14-16).

The betrayal by a member of Jesus' inner circle is no surprise. Matthew tips off the reader in 10:4 and discloses the traitor's identity as Judas Iscariot. Among the Gospels, however, Matthew highlights Judas's role and discusses his fate more than the other Gospel writers do. Judas's identity, motive, and perspective continue to fascinate people today. He has been the subject of recent scholarly/cultural debate on the heels of an alleged "lost" book associated with him, and such information fuels greater speculation. (For two perspectives, see N. T. Wright, *The Gospel of Judas: Have We Missed the Truth about Christianity?* [Grand Rapids: Baker Books, 2006] and Bart D. Ehrman, *The Lost Gospel of Judas Iscariot: a New Look at Betrayer and Betrayed* [New York: Oxford University Press, 2006].)

From Matthew's perspective, Judas's motives are unclear. It is possible that his surname "Iscariot," the root of which comes from the same word we use for "dagger," indicates a link to revolutionaries. Matthew does not clarify this, nor does he give the reader insight into the traditional views that Judas was a "greedy" disciple or the keeper of the treasury.

The Gospel writer indicates that Judas was responsible for two things. He revealed the time and location of Jesus' private place of prayer to the religious authorities so that they could arrest him without disturbing the peace. Then, when they arrived, he kissed Jesus to identify him in the crowd among faces covered by darkness (Brown, *Death of Jesus,* 1:242-43).

Judas did not betray Jesus' identity. Jesus was well known to the people and the authorities and had no fear of appearing in public. In previous sessions, we learned that Jesus taught openly in the court of the Gentiles about the futility of the temple and about his role as the returning Bridegroom. Judas also did not give the temple authorities secret information about Jesus' plans. Jesus spoke openly about his future.

The issue, however, relates to the Roman authorities and their fear of riots. If the temple police arrested Jesus during the day, the crowds would react, and the Romans would be disturbed. Apparently, the time and location eluded the authorities enough that the only way to gain access to Jesus quietly was to bribe one of the inner circle. They needed Judas so they could find Jesus under the cloak of darkness and locate him quickly in the shadows (Brown, *Death of Jesus,* 2:1401).

Another disciple denied that he knew Jesus. As he did with Judas, Jesus anticipated what would happen and told Peter about it (26:31-35).

As we have noted before, Peter's stature grows in Matthew. He comes a long way from his stumble out of the boat on lack of faith (14:29) to announce Jesus' identity correctly (16:16). Just as quickly as Peter understood Jesus, though, he also misinterpreted Jesus' role. He did not want Jesus to die (16:22) and assumed that Elijah and Moses had returned for a long visit on the mountain (17:4).

In these scenes, the impetuous disciple retreats to the campfire in Caiaphas's courtyard (26:69-75). When confronted, Peter denies Jesus three times but does not accept money for the act. He returns to Jesus and does not suffer the same fate as Judas.

THE DISCIPLES (26:20)

The disciples appeared together and collapsed as a team. They did not understand the act of the woman who poured perfume on Jesus; they fell asleep while Jesus prayed; they attempted to defend Jesus with swords; and they abandoned him during trial.

Events in the Darkness

TWO LAST MEALS WITH FRIENDS (26:6-30)

The last events began with two final meals. The first took place in Bethany at the home of Simon the leper (26:6-13). Jesus' choice of a leper and the response of the unnamed woman take the reader back to Jesus' vision of the kingdom (5:1-12). He ate with a meek individual, and a scorned woman anointed him for burial. These are examples of people to whom Jesus wished to extend hospitality, and they behaved like model citizens in his kingdom.

Unnamed disciples made preparations for the second meal (26:17-30). The Passover meal followed the practices of a Greco-Roman symposium. The men "reclined" at a square table, lying on couches that could hold twelve (or, in this case, thirteen) men. They propped themselves with their left elbows and used their right hands to eat. They surrounded the table on three sides; the host sat in the center. The fourth side, opposite the host, was open for the waiters to serve the meal.

They ate the traditional meal of the Jewish Passover, with elements that reminded them of the journey out of Egypt. The two-course meal began with food and finished with wine, singing, or storytelling. In this case, Jesus shared the food, took the bread, and used it as a symbol for his body. The wine symbolized his blood and the anticipated banquet in the heavenly kingdom. Instead of storytelling, the meal concluded with a hymn.

ARREST AND BETRAYAL BY A "FRIEND" IN A GARDEN (26:31-55)

When Jesus arrived at the Mount of Olives with his disciples, he predicted Peter's denial (26:31-35). From there, he took Peter, James, and John to Gethsemane. Ignoring the urgency of Jesus' request (v. 38), the disciples slept while he prayed alone. After the third attempt at urging the disciples to pray with him, Jesus awakened them to greet his betrayer (v. 46). Judas, who assumed responsibility of the situation, kissed Jesus to identify the person to arrest.

A greater hand was at work because the events fulfilled a larger plan. Jesus addressed Judas as "friend," a term used only two other times in Matthew, both in parables. In the parable of the vineyard, the householder addresses a complaining laborer: "My friend, I am not being unfair to you" (20:13). In the parable of the wedding banquet, a last-minute guest is not properly attired. The king, the host, asks, "My friend, how do you come here to be without clothes?" (22:12-13). In both cases, the "friend" is the object of rebuke and judgment. Judas exhibited the same qualities as the "friends" in both parables (Parsons, "Commentary," 156-57). Judas thought he was in charge, but his decision to betray his teacher resulted in the fulfillment of a greater purpose.

TRIAL IN CAIAPHAS'S COURT (26:57-68)

Just as the scene opened with a plot to arrest Jesus, the focus returns to the courtyard of Caiaphas. The high priest presided over the sitting Jewish religious council. The Sanhedrin was a loose coalition of priests, elders, the high priest's family, and wealthy influential Jews. They functioned as a judicial body on behalf of the Roman government (Brown, *Death of Jesus,* 1:339). Although there is some debate, likely this was an informal meeting of the religious establishment, convened to poll the group to see if they could execute their plans. Under the guise of an informal meeting or hearing, the members of the Sanhedrin would not have needed to follow their own rules (Blevins, "Trial of Jesus," 931-32).

Two witnesses provided the only evidence against Jesus, a charge of threatening to tear down the temple. The high priest questioned Jesus about his identity: "Tell us if you are the Messiah, the Son of God" (26:63). Jesus' obscure answer, "You have said so," concluded with an apocalyptic prediction of a return: "But I tell you from now on, you will see the Son of Man seated at the right hand of Power coming on the clouds of heaven." The high priest countered by charging him with blasphemy, echoing the earlier words of the religious leaders in Capernaum (9:3; see session 4). The trial concluded with slapping and hitting.

DENIAL BY THE CAMPFIRE (26:69-75)

Thus far in some of the most dramatic moments in Matthew, the unknown strangers like the leper and a woman behave like the closest friends of Jesus. His daily companions, his disciples, do not follow through on their commitments. The same happens for the ostensible leader of the disciples, Peter. At the meal, Peter insisted that he would stay with Jesus. Now in the heat of the moment, by the glow of a campfire, he denies knowing Jesus.

The contrast between Peter and Jesus is notable. Peter, the model disciple, fell asleep three times in prayer; Jesus prayed three times and gained strength. Peter denied knowing him three times, while Jesus answered three charges brought before him (Boring, "Matthew," 481).

Peter acted more like the betrayer Judas. Although he was not paid to do so, he disassociated himself with Jesus, fulfilling another prediction of betrayal. He swore an oath disavowing Jesus.

SUICIDE IN THE CEMETERY (27:1-10)

The closing scene of this section recounts the tragic end of Jesus' betrayer. The religious leaders condemned Jesus, and Judas was aware of his fate. Sensing the weight of his treachery, Judas did not turn to Jesus for forgiveness; he went instead to the high priest looking for redemption. Ironically, the old administrators of the sacrificial system failed to mete out forgiveness. Their pawn, Judas, was caught in his own tangled web. Even though he confessed to his priest (v. 4), they rejected him. Judas chose the wrong group with whom to ally. He chose evil over the kingdom of heaven, and he paid the price. Overwhelmed with guilt, he committed suicide (Boring, "Matthew," 484).

A greater plan continued. Through his personal choices, one in Jesus' inner circle fulfilled a prophecy from Jeremiah (18:2; 32:7-9).

Darkness Reveals Everything

Few things are ever what they seem in the Gospels or in life. The people expected to remain with Jesus denied him, and those responsible for his death actually gave life to the world. Dark places became the staging ground for both incidents. We expect to see best in the light, but spiritually we understand better when we pay attention to what the darkness reveals.

THE DIFFERENCE BETWEEN LOYALTY AND TREACHERY

The only way to distinguish between loyalty and treachery is to watch behavior in the darkness. For friends who followed Jesus from the beginning, darkness was a cruel enemy. Jesus' second to last day on earth was one of the worst for his companions. His friends became traitors, and he was left to face a mock trial alone. Jesus' table, a symbol of friendship and community throughout the Gospel, became the gathering place for the loyal and disloyal. The unknown woman, who spent the least amount of time with Jesus, expressed uncommon loyalty and understanding. Those who knew

him best (the disciples) or heard his teachings (the religious authorities) played key roles in Jesus' execution.

JESUS' IDENTITY AS THE SON OF GOD

Caiaphas answers the question that has been with us since Jesus first
told the disciples to keep quiet (16:20). He is the "Son of God." For
the first time publicly, a human spoke the good news without rebuttal, and he made the statement at the epicenter of Jewish religious
power.

Jesus is not afraid of the darkness. The dark places like a garden,
Caiaphas's court, or a campfire reveal our true hearts. In these
places, Judas, Caiaphas, and Peter reveal their motives—but they are
also the points where light breaks in (4:16) and judgment is served
(8:12). No amount of time spent with Jesus or familiarity with his
teachings can prepare one for the tests in the dark. These experiences always come.

GOD'S ULTIMATE PLAN

We see God's plan at work in the darkness. The enemies of Jesus
thought they could hide their trial from the people and bring him
out in the light to hear the cries of "Crucify" the next day. In the
dark, however, God knew the enemies' schemes and used these
plans to bring in the kingdom. They "secretly" plotted to kill Jesus,
but Jesus was really the one who knew the outcome. Their presence
fit a larger plan to conquer evil and for Jesus to be raised from the
dead. The evil ones fulfill a greater purpose. They would be duped
by their own schemes.

These scenes remind us of the words Jesus spoke in 10:16-42.
He explained then, and it was now fulfilled, that the disciples would
face their worst enemies in darkness. Whatever was hidden, whispered, or shaded would become visible.

Conclusion

The question remains for the reader of this episode of first-century
Law and Order: who is on trial? The authorities successfully arrested
Jesus and convened a mock hearing against him. In reality, the religious authorities and the disciples were the ones on trial. The
question asked by the prosecutor (Jesus) was this: "Do you recognize who I am?"

Peter's accusers around the campfire questioned him. He failed miserably because he denied the intimate knowledge.

Judas knew the answer to the question but turned to the religious leaders for assistance. He was found guilty, and he punished himself for his crime.

The religious leaders heard the answer to their question, "Are you the Son God?" They had no more excuses; they heard this information confirmed publicly without rebuttal. Jesus promised to return with power and authority.

In the ultimate twist, Jesus placed his own accusers, friends, and followers on trial. Guilty as charged.

1. The plan of God is accomplished with God's initiative as Son of God and the human response of evil and denial. How have the events in your life been the result of God's providence and your choices?

_____

_____

_____

_____

_____

_____

2. Many passages of Scripture use light as the arena for God's work. In these passages, God works at night. What does this mean for the choices we make when no one is watching? How does darkness become a place for God to do good work? Are there dark places in life where God is already working?

_____

_____

_____

_____

_____

_____

3. Life is not nearly as predictable as we assume. There are many twists and turns. What can we learn about treachery from the lessons of Peter's and Judas's story?

_____

_____

_____

_____

_____

_____

4. What is the difference between Peter's and Judas's responses? Why did one return to the fold of disciples and another commit suicide?

_____

_____

_____

_____

_____

_____

5. The people who appeared to spend the most time with Jesus or had the most information were often not the most loyal or trustworthy. What does this say about faith and belief today? How are loyalty and fidelity taught?

_____

_____

_____

_____

_____

_____

6. How is God's redeeming presence made evident in times of pain when God seems absent?

_____

_____

_____

_____

7. Watch this scene from *The Visual Bible* DVD: disc 2, 1:50:00–1:56:18. How does the character of Jesus place the Sanhedrin on trial? Discuss the differences between Peter's and Judas's treachery.

_____

_____

_____

_____

_____

_____

Apocalyptic Death

When people die, things are revealed. Any life, no matter how large or small, affects another person. Consider how people react in similar ways to the deaths of close loved ones and famous people. We remember where we were when we received the news. We share stories and learn more about the deceased person than we knew before. We discuss the times that quickly passed and recall events long forgotten. Death has a way of disclosing more about a person than we knew in life.

In Matthew's story, the events accompanying Jesus' death reveal a deeper meaning to his life that some people had not seen. Jesus' death unveils his identity as Son of God for all to see, begins a new day in humanity's relationship with God, and demonstrates how people and nature react to him.

Apocalyptic Themes in Matthew

Matthew describes Jesus' death as an apocalyptic event. The word *apocalyptic*, literally "unveiling," denotes events that have been hidden but are now revealed. Much like a curtain rising to open a play or a door opening to reveal a secret passageway, apocalyptic events are the visual signs that indicate new beginnings.

This imagery occurs throughout the Old Testament. Books such as Daniel, Amos, Habbakuk, and Ezekiel use apocalyptic themes to express the hopes and fears of the faithful. Six apocalyptic characteristics are noteworthy (Brown, *Death of Jesus*, 2:1120-21).

(1) Persecution and/or death of faithful people. In Daniel 3:12, Shadrach, Meschach, and Abednego are persecuted for not bowing down to a golden idol.

(2) Blessing on those who believed in God. In Daniel 12:12-13, those who faithfully endure persecution are blessed.

(3) Judgment on those who rejected God. In Isaiah 65:11-13, people who commit evil against the people of God receive punishment.

(4) Heavenly signs and wonders. In Amos 8:9, we learn that the sun will be darkened, indicating the day of the Lord is near.

(5) Earthly signs and wonders. Several things occur on the earth. Zechariah 14:5 describes an earthquake. In Ezekiel 37:10-13, the prophet speaks to dead bones, they come to life, and the tombs open. According to the prophet, when these events happen, the people will know that God is intervening.

(6) Gentiles who responded to God's work. In Isaiah 60:6, Gentiles ride camels from faraway lands to praise God.

These signs were multi-sensory experiences, and believers preserved the images verbally through the pages of the Hebrew Bible and visually in murals. In a synagogue in Dura-Europas from the third century AD, archaeologists discovered murals of Old Testament scenes including, as we noted in session 1, Ezekiel's prophecy of dead bones living and the tombs opening. The hopes of Ezekiel carried well past Matthew's day. As the people worshiped, they imagined these events being fulfilled in their time.

In this passage in Matthew, apocalyptic signs have cosmic significance. These wonders reveal a new beginning in God's relationship with humanity. Through divine intervention, God begins anew with all creation. The world responds positively and negatively to the event, and a number of apocalyptic themes follow.

An innocent man is persecuted and dies, and this person is God's Son. Those who believe in Jesus are blessed; those who reject Jesus receive judgment. Some Gentiles respond positively to Jesus. The heavens and the earth react.

Responses to Jesus' Conviction, Crucifixion, and Death

At first glance, Matthew's account of Jesus' crucifixion and death is similar to that of Mark. We read little about how he was crucified—simply that it happened (27:35). Jesus speaks once on the cross (27:46) and cries out when he dies (27:50).

We do not hear the conversation between Jesus and the two thieves (as Luke shares), nor do we hear much from the mouth of Jesus. Luke and John contain most of the traditional "seven last words of Christ."

The Gospel of Matthew focuses on the apocalyptic imagery that occurs during the crucifixion. These signs were familiar to listeners steeped in Jewish tradition.

PILATE, THE AUTHORITIES, AND PILATE'S WIFE RESPONDED TO JESUS' CONVICTION (27:11-37, 62-66)

Pilate and the authorities frame this passage. The scenes open with Pilate's questioning Jesus' title and close with Pilate's attempting to secure the tomb.

Pilate attempted to absolve himself of responsibility for Jesus' sentence. Despite attempts to wash his hands of innocent blood (27:24), Pilate's words betrayed the truth. He knew Jesus was the rightful heir to the throne of David (27:14), and his rhetorical question revealed that he knew Jesus was innocent: "What shall I do with this man?" (27:23).

The Jewish authorities were just as guilty. They cried out for Barabbas, stripped and scourged Jesus, and incited the crowds to mock and jeer him (27:20). When Jesus hung on the cross, they joined with the crowd's derision (27:41). After Jesus was buried, they returned to Pilate and sealed their fate (27:62).

The Roman authorities were equally complicit. The soldiers stripped him of his clothes, jeered him, and offered him vinegar to drink. Presumably, they nailed Jesus to the cross. They gambled over the clothes they stripped off him (27:34-36).

Despite these negative responses from Jewish and Gentile authorities, one Gentile woman provided the first positive response to Jesus' death and the first apocalyptic sign. Pilate's wife intervened on Jesus' behalf. She sent a message: "Have nothing to do with that innocent man, for today I have suffered a great deal because of a dream about him." Her dream was an indicator of divine intervention. Just as the magi were warned in a dream not to return to Herod (2:12), Pilate's wife warned her husband about crucifying Jesus. Pilate rejected her advice; but as a Gentile, she was the first sign that something new was about to happen (27:19) (Garland, *Reading Matthew*, 257). (David Garland notes the ways this woman has been treated throughout the history of the church. In this case, I view her positively as a sign and agent of change.)

THE CROWDS AND BYSTANDERS MOCKED JESUS' CRUCIFIXION (27:38-44)

When Jesus was on trial, the crowds followed the hypnotic orders of the religious authorities and requested the release of the notorious bandit Barabbas. Around the cross, they humiliated Jesus. In 27:43, their words reveal their knowledge of Jesus' identity: "If you are the son of God . . . ."

Ironically, if Jesus had done as they asked, he would not be the Son of God as he claimed. To show his relationship with the Father, he had to complete the task and die (Brown, *Death of Jesus,* 996).

THE HEAVENS POINTED TO THE SIGNIFICANCE OF JESUS' DEATH (27:45-50)

With the exception of Pilate's wife, thus far the reactions to Jesus' death have been negative. The people rejected and crucified him. When darkness descends, the mood of the text changes. Even though darkness portends gloom for the enemies of Jesus, the heavens point to hope for those who accept Jesus.

Under the cloak of darkness, Jesus spoke from the cross. The words, "My God, my God, why have you forsaken me?" echo Psalm 22:2. God had not forsaken Jesus, however, because the apocalyptic signs and wonders indicated that God intervened. Jesus did express this human cry during the worst agony of all, a feeling of distance and isolation from God. Jesus' last act was to cry out with a loud voice and yield his spirit voluntarily to God.

THE EARTH REACTED TO JESUS' DEATH (27:51-53)

The next apocalyptic signs occurred on the earth. The curtain of the temple tore, the earth shook, tombs opened, dead believers were alive, and the saints appeared to other people. The action in the temple echoed Jesus' earlier prediction that the temple would be destroyed (24:1-2). The earthquake was reminiscent of the one described in Zechariah. The believers, empty tombs, and public appearances fulfilled Ezekiel's hope in the valley of dry bones. The believers remained in the cemetery following the resurrection.

BELIEVERS RESPONDED TO JESUS' DEATH (27:54-61)

Three sets of believers responded positively to Jesus' death. The first, a "centurion and those who were with him," presumably soldiers, completed the apocalyptic portrait. Another Gentile, like Pilate's wife, accepted Jesus and announced as truth the mockery at the foot of the cross: "Truly this man was God's Son!" (27:54)

Other Jewish believers responded just as appropriately. The first was a group of Jewish women: Mary Magdalene, Mary the Mother of James and Joseph, and the mother of James and John, the sons of Zebedee.

A wealthy man was the last believer to respond in this sequence. Joseph of Arimathea, a disciple outside the circle of the Twelve, received permission from Pilate to bury Jesus' body. He showed the ultimate honor in Jewish society. He treated Jesus as if he were his own father, cutting the tomb and burying the body.

Summary

Several apocalyptic elements are prominent in the passage. The Jewish authorities, the crowds, and the Roman authorities persecute and crucify an innocent man. Cosmic events ensue. The skies grow dark, the temple curtain tears, the earth quakes, tombs open, dead bodies are alive, and eyewitnesses see them. Gentiles become the vehicle through which God communicates (Pilate's wife) and believe in Jesus as the Son of God (centurion). Because Jesus is identified not merely as an innocent person but also as the Son of God publicly and privately, and because people recognize this throughout the story, terrible consequences result when they reject him. All who reject Jesus are judged for their deeds. Those who believe in Jesus are blessed.

What Jesus' Death Reveals in Matthew

Apocalyptic events disclose information. The meaning of the word apocalyptic, "unveiling," implies that something previously hidden is no longer secretive. In this story, the public wonders, signs, and transformations that are felt, seen, and heard pull the curtain back. Witnesses have the chance to discover what is happening.

Matthew does not reveal, however, how Jesus was crucified. In comparison with other accounts or a modern portrayal of his death in films like *The Passion of the Christ*, Matthew does not mention the blood or many other gory details. Jesus died. That is enough information. To get into these details distracts from the message of the cross and causes the reader to engage in scientific or psychological analysis of the text.

The Gospel does show that everyone had a chance to see God's revelation in Christ. God was not trying to keep anything hidden about Jesus. In case anyone doubted, the apocalyptic elements pointed the way. The signs cut across ethnic, religious, social, gender, and economic barriers. Gentiles, Jews, rich, poor, disciples, and outcasts—everyone is represented in the story. All have the chance to see the bodies and the darkness and feel the earthquake.

What do these signs reveal? Matthew reveals that Jesus' death was not a well-kept secret. He predicted it, described it, and prepared the disciples for it. His identification as the Son of God was also known. Even his accusers used the title whether or not they believed it.

The apocalyptic elements in Matthew show that the kingdom of heaven began officially when Jesus died. In Jesus' day, most people assumed that the kingdom would begin at a later time and still longed for it to come. But God did not even wait for the resurrection to reverse the effects of death (Boring, "Matthew," 496). Jesus' sacrificial death fulfilled the hopes of prophets who used specific imagery to inspire believers. Through Jesus' death, a new day dawned. Faithful Jewish believers who were dead rose from tombs.

Jesus' death revealed that the kingdom did not come through violent military overthrow, civil disobedience, or rapid judgment of all non-Jewish people. Instead, the kingdom began slowly with the violent, sacrificial death of the innocent Son of God and will not be completely inaugurated until his return.

The death of Jesus in Matthew then is both triumph and tragedy. Triumphantly, Jesus conquered death through the cross and completed the picture of forgiveness that he explained at the Passover meal with the disciples. This death was for the forgiveness of sins.

For those who believe that he is the Son of God, there is great blessing and hope. In Matthew, God communicates through some unlikely sources, especially Pilate's wife. She functions much like the magi, Gentiles who represent hope. Because the new kingdom of heaven is not fully complete, there is still time for people to believe. The centurion is just one example. This persecutor of Jesus became a believer.

Jesus' death is tragic for people who reject him as the Son of God. Everyone could see and feel the apocalyptic signs, but not all understood their meaning, associated their occurrence with Jesus, or reacted to Jesus' death with belief. The Roman authorities saw the portents and refused to believe. They responded by trying to prevent further divine intervention and disruptions of power.

What Jesus' Death Reveals Today

Just as everyone who actually saw Jesus responded, so today the public display of Jesus' death and the supernatural signs and wonders evoke a response in people. One cannot read about the cross and the accompanying signs without reacting. Like the apocalyptic events in the Old Testament, now believers in Jesus find encouragement and instruction for living and a new image of God's love. Four themes are revealed from behind the curtain.

THE VISIBILITY OF THE CROSS

People cannot avoid the cross. Jesus' death is so visible that everyone confronted by the cross must make a decision to accept or reject him.

God offered everyone forgiveness of sins through Jesus' death. All people, regardless of ethnicity, social or economic status, or background can access God's message. Even a centurion who responded with fear believed. Everyone has the opportunity to see that Jesus is "Son of God." Those who understand his identity find hope.

THE PRESENCE OF GOD IN SUFFERING AND SACRIFICE

One popular explanation of the question, "My God, my God, why have you forsaken me?" is that God "turned his back" on his Son. The danger of this interpretation is in its portrayal of God. When carried to its logical conclusion, if God turned away from his perfect Son when carrying the weight of sin on the cross, then God certainly turns away from us when displeased.

Matthew indicates, however, that God is always present in suffering, especially in the moment of the greatest sacrifice. Jesus wanted God's presence on the cross as he did in the garden of Gethsemane when he said, "Let this cup pass from me." This does not mean, however, that God stood by as a casual observer or turned away.

Jesus' journey to the cross provides the ultimate encouragement for believers facing dire circumstances. God did not forsake his Son, and Jesus endured abuse and the rejection of humanity. No one will ever have to face this kind of rejection again.

THE FUTILITY OF HUMAN INSTITUTIONS

Jesus' death reveals the best and worst humanity can offer. Only one man has the power to conquer death. The rest simply show their lust for power and control. In the end, even the best representatives the world can offer—its religious and political leaders—can succumb. Institutions, whether governmental or ecclesiastical, typically turn inward when confronted with Jesus' death (Boring, "Matthew," 498).

Jesus offered a different way of non-retaliation. He went willingly to his death without attempting to strike back. He urged the disciples to put away their swords and endured the punishment of Jews and Gentiles. When faced with disappointment and persecution, the appropriate response is a sacrificial life. Believers in the power of the cross do not need to resort to violence because Jesus has conquered the effects of persecution and death.

By contrast, consider the initial reaction of religious and political leaders to the message of nonviolence and sacrifice during times of grave injustice. During the civil rights period in America, terrorism in Northern Ireland, and apartheid in South Africa, religious and political leaders protected one another from change. Preachers invoked Scriptures to justify their actions, and politicians protected the system they controlled. The message of sacrificial death was a great stumbling block. The experiences revealed the danger of trust in human institutions—rather than the message of Christ—for salvation.

DEATH IS TEMPORARY

The last word in life is not death. Raising bodies from the tombs, God began to reverse the effects of death before Jesus was resurrected. Because Jesus confronted death, believers can face their own mortality long before the event occurs. We receive every day as a gift and live knowing that the pain of suffering and death will not stop God's forgiveness and new life.

Living in light of Jesus' death allows believers to behave honestly and transparently. Jesus always revealed his plans to his inner circle and in the last week explained to everyone what was about to occur. Upon reflection, his death came as no surprise and the apocalyptic nature of the events revealed the mysteries that once seemed secret.

Our response to troubles with family, friends, or society can be transparency and honesty. Secrets taken to the grave become the curses of the next generation. Openness in light of Christ's sacrifice brings light to dark places. Funerals that were once events of tragedy can become services of memories, hope, and forgiveness. We can even find hope at a funeral. Death is difficult, but our mortality is not the last word. Faith in the power of Jesus' death reverses the effects that the end of life has on the rest of life. Believers react to death with hope, knowing that we can experience the forgiveness of sins and can endure the pain of loss.

Conclusion

How we react to death, especially the death of Jesus, reveals our understanding of Jesus as the Son of God. His death must evoke more than pity; we must respond with a yes or no to his identity. We demonstrate that response through human emotion and faithful actions.

In C. S. Lewis's *The Lion, the Witch, and the Wardrobe*, Lucy and Susan react to the death of Aslan much like the centurion, Joseph of Arimathea, and the women responded to Jesus' death. After the witch departs to prepare for battle, Lewis writes,

> At this moment the children were for a few seconds in very great danger. For with wild cries and a noise of skirling pipes and shrill horns blowing, the whole of the vile rabble came sweeping off the hill-top and down the slope right past their hiding-place. They felt the Spectres go by them like a cold wind and they felt the ground shake beneath them under the galloping feet of the Minotaurs; and overhead there went a flurry of foul wings and a blackness of vultures and giant bats. At any other time they would have trembled with fear; but now the sadness and shame and horror of Aslan's death so filled their minds that they hardly thought of it. . . . If you've been up all night and cried till you have no more tears left in you—you will know there comes in the end a sort of quietness. You feel as if nothing is ever going to happen again. At any rate that was how it felt to these two. (159)

Apocalyptic Death

1. What did the cross reveal to people watching?

_____

_____

_____

_____

_____

_____

2. Secrets are often brought to light immediately during or following funerals. Sometimes these memories are positive, others negative. What does Jesus' death on the cross reveal to us about keeping secrets? How should we communicate with loved ones now so that they do not have to hear the truth later?

_____

_____

_____

_____

_____

_____

3. How is the cross both triumphant and tragic today?

_____

_____

_____

_____

_____

_____

4. In the cross, God can be viewed as the harsh punitive Lord bringing wrath on the world, or God's love can be seen through a sacrificial life. Which image does Matthew portray? What words and terms can be used today to describe this image of God to others?

_____

_____

_____

_____

_____

5. In the cross, sacrifice brings in the kingdom of God, not violence. How can believers respond sacrificially to a violent world? What steps must be taken to change the rhetoric and behavior of violence? What should a believer's role be as an instrument of peace?

_____

_____

_____

_____

_____

_____

6. Watch the crucifixion scene from *The Passion of the Christ* DVD (chapter 27, 1:34:45–1:45:45; dir. Mel Gibson, Hollywood, Icon Productions, Twentieth-Century Fox Home Entertainment, 2004). Compare Matthew's portrayal of the act of crucifixion with the scene in Gibson's film. Which one is more graphic?

_____

_____

_____

_____

_____

_____

Apocalyptic Death

Reports of the Resurrection

Matthew 28:1-15
Focal text—Matthew 28:1-15

If Jesus had a "stomping grounds," it was Galilee. This was the place where everything started for Jesus. He grew up in Nazareth, he made his home in Capernaum, and the place where Peter declared him to be the Christ was in Caesarea-Philippi. All of these places were within Galilee.

If Galilee was the first place where people actually saw Jesus do some of the most miraculous things, and if it was the place where he started his ministry with a bang, it was also where he first struggled. In Gadara, some Gentiles asked him to leave (8:34); and in Capernaum, the religious leaders accused him of blasphemy (9:3). In his hometown of Nazareth, the people first plotted against him. They railed against him following his homecoming sermon in the Nazareth synagogue. They said, "Isn't this the carpenter? Isn't this Mary's son and the brother of James?" (Matt 13:53-58). The opposition was so bad that Jesus could not heal anyone in that area. They doubted his power and turned away from him. He left there to go to Jerusalem. They turned away from him again just as they did in Galilee.

In Matthew 28, everything has changed. This is resurrection Sunday. The past is over, and a bright future dawns. Matthew 28 answers the question of how the message should be reported and where the good news can be shared.

How the Resurrection Was Reported

The text indicates three different ways of telling the story. One report comes from heaven (28:5), the second personally from Jesus (28:8), and the third from the guards (28:11).

AN ANGEL DESCENDED FROM HEAVEN (28:1-7)

Two Marys, Mary Magdalene and another woman, visited the tomb, but something had occurred. Matthew does not describe the event of the resurrection of Jesus. There are no live-action eyewitness reports. The women went to the tomb that morning to do their duty and discovered that the resurrection had already occurred. The emphasis is on the events that confirm the resurrection. The earth shook, much like it did apocalyptically at the cross. The quake pointed to the power of life rather than the power of death. The angel descended, removed the stone, stunned the guards, and awaited the women. In Matthew 1, the angel reassured Joseph in a dream. This messenger descends to announce the news of the resurrection.

When the women reached the tomb, they were afraid but not stunned like the guards. They listened to the angel. The messenger knew who they were looking for and told them the news: "He is not here, for he has risen." The angel instructed them to see the empty place and to tell the disciples to meet Jesus in Galilee.

JESUS CONFIRMED THE MESSAGE (28:8-10)

The women left the place with responses of fear and joy. On their way, Jesus appeared bodily for the first time. When they saw him, they grabbed his feet and worshiped him.

Although their response seems strange to the modern reader, Greco-Roman literature indicates that taking hold of one's feet was a sign of love. For instance, in the popular ancient novel *Chariton*, a father embraces Chareas while a mother grabs his knees, weeping in front of a large group of people (*Chariton* 3.5.3). This same gesture occurs when Paul says farewell to the Ephesian congregation in Acts 20. They embrace his knees.

Coupled with worship, the actions demonstrate love, deference, respect, honor, and reverence. In Matthew, this is the second time Jesus has allowed people to worship him since his birth as a baby. In the temptation in the desert, he mentioned worshiping God, but in the boat (14:33) and here, worship of him is the equivalent of worshiping God (Garland, *Reading Matthew*, 264). Jesus responded with terms of endearment (28:10) for his "brothers," the disciples who abandoned him, and gave the women instructions similar to the angel's: to tell the disciples to go to Galilee.

GUARDS TOLD THE FACTS (28:11)

After rousing from their slumber, some of the guards decided to report what they saw. They were the only male eyewitnesses present who could have possibly seen the resurrection and the angel's descent. They responded with fear appropriately, but they lacked an ingredient. They did not or could not listen to the angel or respond to the event in worship and submission. They could have been like the centurion who witnessed Jesus' death and understood his identity. Instead, their words merely retold the facts of the case rather than announcing a life-transforming expression of faith.

Where the Resurrection Was Reported

One expects that the religious leadership would be open to the announcement that someone had conquered death. Safely headquartered in Jerusalem, the religious leaders received such news. But this place reflected its old problems of power and authority; the best place to share news of a resurrection was elsewhere.

JERUSALEM (28:11-15)

The only eyewitnesses present at the resurrection relayed the story, but they were quickly met with opposition. The chief priests' response indicates how true the resurrection is. If the event did not occur, a cover-up would be unnecessary. The religious leaders need a conspiracy theory to cover their tracks. The cost of the conspiracy is more than the betrayal (28:13-14) (Garland, *Reading Matthew*, 264).

GALILEE

The only place left to report the events was Galilee, but problems existed. Three days earlier, sinful, angry people had rejected the disciples and rushed them from a garden area into a mock trial. Seven days earlier, they proclaimed Jesus king, and a few months earlier they were in Galilee. It's possible that the people in Galilee were skeptical. They were the ones who first accused him of blasphemy (9:3); they started the problems; they turned against them; they mocked the family. Would they possibly reject them again?

Matthew explains that Jesus had a different strategy, and it began with the resurrection. The disciples had lingered too long at the epicenter of Jewish politics and religion. Even though Jewish people were still welcome, they needed to get away from Jerusalem and Judea to hear a new beginning. In Matthew 10, Jesus told the disciples to focus only on the house of Israel. Now the temple veil had been torn, and everyone was welcome into the kingdom. Galilee was the natural place for this to begin. Because of its association with Gentiles and because Jesus encountered Gentiles in this region, Galilee fit the plan perfectly.

Jesus returned to the very people who rejected him and asked those people to follow him out of the tomb. People knew him so well that when he appeared with a resurrected body, they quickly associated the new body with the old one. They had touched his body before in this place, and they would understand its significance now.

Jesus began in Galilee and placed people from that region in charge of the movement. He demonstrated that even though people rejected him, disobedient people could still be leaders in the mission.

How to Report a Resurrection

The nature of the reporting and the location of the message are significant in resurrection faith. A person can believe the facts but still miss the significance of the event. According to Matthew, the guards and religious leaders knew the resurrection had occurred; otherwise, they would not have tried to cover it up. The question in the Gospel is always "What will people do with the information?" The women demonstrate for believers today the kinds of qualities necessary for resurrection faith. This faith acknowledges more than an empty tomb. An individual expresses this faith through worship, relationship, courage, and testimony.

WORSHIP (28:9)

We have noted that the one quality missing in the soldiers was their worship of the risen Christ. The women demonstrated it through nonverbal gestures. They understood that Jesus was the Son of God, and they served him only (Matt 4:10).

Believers today serve that which they worship. Worshiping a risen Savior, placing Jesus' values above others, is reflected in a life that imitates his sacrificial qualities.

RELATIONSHIP (28:10)

The women not only demonstrated their loyalty but had an experience of Jesus' living presence with them. The disciples were part of the new faith family. They were still the "brothers" of Jesus. The familial language implies a sense of reciprocity. As they experienced Jesus, they did not serve as slaves; they knew him intimately as friend and guide. Jesus completes the picture of the images of God Matthew has painted throughout the book. Jesus is the loving Son (17:5), faithful bridegroom (9:15; 12:49; 22:1-14), and brother (12:49; 28:10).

People who have resurrection faith live in relationship with Jesus just as they do with a loving father, devoted sibling, or a faithful spouse. Even through mistakes (like the denial of Peter), there is still a chance for forgiveness, redemption, and ongoing communication.

COURAGE

The disciples returned to the familiar faces of Galilee as courageous people. They went there not only by faith in the angel's report but also because they knew Jesus would meet them. Because he went ahead of them, they knew his living presence would walk beside them as they confronted people who doubted.

When people are fired from jobs or kicked out of a family of origin, the last place they want to go for retraining or reunion is the old job or home place. They certainly would not want to invite these people back into their lives to assist them as they raise their kids or train future generations.

Resurrection faith gives believers the courage to go back to places of fear, rejection, bitterness, anger, and hostility. The believer returns to serve someone who has rejected her and to enlist more help in the movement of God.

We can talk about saying to enemies, "We love you" (Matt 5:44). Jesus sent the disciples one step further. They were not merely going back to the world to announce that he was risen; they were going back to a place that despised them to say, "The risen life is part of my life. I want to try to start over again, and you are the ones I want in my life."

Ironically, that is what Jesus did for the disciples. He did not start over with new ones; he did not convert old followers; he started with the remaining Jewish disciples and began to rebuild.

The same thing happens for believers who fail today. Jesus does not say, "Well, they sinned. I'm starting over with a new group or a new church." Much like the genealogy that opens the book of Matthew, the failures of today become links in the spiritual chain.

Jesus comes right back to us where we are and says, "I'm here, I'm risen, and I want you to be a part of my movement called the church."

TESTIMONY

Reporting is a part of resurrection faith, but the message is more than "just the facts." The story is so compelling that it prevents cover-up, slander, or bribery. We share this message through daily lives of obedience to Christ's way. As we follow the instructions and imitate his life, we demonstrate to others the difference the resurrection faith makes in life.

One Easter Sunday morning my church in San Angelo, Texas, planned to feature a soloist dressed in biblical costume as Mary Magdalene. She sang "I Saw the Lord," reflecting the account in Matthew; it was the highlight of the worship service. After the service, I thanked her for the performance.

The woman said, "You'll never believe what happened to me. I was standing in the foyer in my costume preparing to enter the sanctuary. I noticed that right after the service began, two guys were standing off to the side in dark suits. None of the ushers were talking to them, and they seemed to be doing nothing. I walked over in my costume and invited them to join us inside the sanctuary for the service. I thought I was being nice, but they looked at me like I was crazy. I said, 'We have a service going on inside; and we'd love to have you join us.'

"They said, 'Ma'am, we can't do that.'

"'Sure you can,' I replied insistently. 'It's Easter; come inside; there's still room for you.'

"One of them walked away and answered his phone. The other one spoke in a stern voice and said,

'Ma'am, we cannot do that because we are Secret Service.'

"I looked at him and said, 'Yeah right, and I'm Mary Magdalene!'

'No, Ma'am,' he replied, 'we are secret service. The president's nephew is here today in the worship service, and we're his security detail. Please step aside.'"

When she told me this story, I could not believe it. The president's nephew was in the service? I checked out her story, and sure enough, one of our church members was dating him, and he flew in to be with her. He decided to come to church that morning for worship. What a marvelous surprise! Immediately I reviewed each point of the sermon and wondered if he stayed awake to hear any of the message.

The real irony in the story occurred to me later that day. I had just finished preaching a sermon on the power of good, amazing, even wonderful news about the most famous person in the world. Another not-so-famous but still relatively popular person with an important surname entered the church, and no one knew until it was too late. If they knew, no one thought it important enough to tell me he was coming! The message of his appearance never made a difference in their behavior. If I had only known, I would have wanted to meet this guest, talk to him, and tell others about him. I preached the entire service and never knew he was there.

Maybe that was the point. The presence of a relative of the president cannot compare to the significance of Jesus' appearance. We cannot keep the most wonderful news about the most significant figure in history to ourselves. If only others could know, then they too might want to talk to him, tell others about him, and worship him. And the best place to start is Galilee.

1. Which is more important—that the resurrection occurred or how the information was reported?

_____

_____

_____

_____

_____

_____

2. Have you ever had wonderful news that you had to keep to yourself? How difficult was it? What makes the difference in the way we share the message of the resurrection?

_____

_____

_____

_____

_____

_____

3. The familial language of "brothers" extended Jesus' relationship to the one who denied him. How is Jesus a "brother" to believers today?

_____

_____

_____

_____

_____

_____

4. Galilee was the place of success and rejection. How do the two go hand in hand? Identify those places in your life. Is it harder or easier to share the message in these places? How do we share the message?

_____

_____

_____

_____

_____

_____

5. Watch this scene from *The Visual Bible* DVD: disc 2, 2:09:50–2:12:20. Compare Jesus' embrace of the women with the text. Does this fit Matthew's portrayal of the reunion between Jesus and the women?

_____

_____

_____

_____

_____

_____

Farewell with Faith

A biography usually concludes by reviewing the person's life and describing the subject's legacy. Ancient biographies ended by reviewing the themes in the story and appealing to the audience to imitate the significant attributes of the person. The Gospel of Matthew places Jesus on a mountain to deliver a brief farewell to the disciples and, by implication, future readers. The setting, instructions, and challenge capture the significance of Matthew's story and show the modern listener how to imitate Jesus' life today. Resurrection faith begins with an experience of Jesus' presence and continues with his presence today.

Farewell from the Mountain

Jesus did not remain on earth to carry out his mission personally. Surprisingly, he left, entrusting his name and legacy to the people who denied and abandoned him. He empowered them with the Trinitarian name to imitate his life throughout the world and invited new people into the faith family. This passage opens with the disciples' seeing Jesus and concludes with the assurance of his presence.

MOUNTAINTOP EXPERIENCES (28:16)

Based on the report of the women, the eleven remaining disciples had enough faith to meet Jesus in Galilee. Like so many times in Jewish history, God met them personally on a mountain.

Mountains were important geographically and theologically. The significant moments in the life of the people's first prophet, Moses, centered on the mountain. In the book of Exodus, mountains provided a location for Moses to work as a shepherd for Jethro

(Exod 3:1); to be reunited with Aaron (4:27); for God to communicate to Moses and give the law (19:2); and for Moses to speak to
the people (19:23). In Deuteronomy, Moses gave his farewell
speech, bestowed authority on Joshua, and died on a mountain
(32:1-50).

As God did through Moses, so Jesus does for the people in
Matthew. The mountains provide important landmarks throughout
the Gospel. Here Jesus faced his last temptation prior to baptism
(4:8); he delivered the great sermon (5:1); he prayed (14:23); he fed
more than 4,000 people (15:29); he was transfigured (17:1); he
spoke of the destruction of the temple (24:3); and he said farewell
(28:16).

RESURRECTION RESPONSE (28:17)

Like the women who first saw Jesus after his resurrection, the disciples completed the portrait of resurrection faith. They worshiped
him, the second time this occurred following resurrection; and they
doubted. Already we have seen that doubt can be a response to the
presence of Christ (14:29) even on the part of faithful disciples.
After the resurrection, doubt was incorporated as an element of
belief.

THE FAITH FAMILY (28:18-20)

With the announcement that Jesus had the authority to empower
the disciples, he sent them down from the mountain with the experience of his presence to continue with them until this new age is
complete. The last time they were together with him, they were told
to keep Jesus' authority quiet (16:20). Now they were empowered
with the ability to move out of the inner circle ("Go") into all the
nations. The Gentiles were welcome, and the disciples must go
where they were rather than expecting the Gentiles to come to
them.

As they went, they were to "disciple" (used here as a verb) new
people into a spiritual family. Two family images have been prevalent throughout the Gospel: spiritual relationships and betrothal.

Matthew opens with a genealogy of which Jesus is a part (1:1-
18). Each person is linked in a human chain of creation, marriage,
and family relationships. Fathers, some wives, two sets of brothers,
and one husband are mentioned. As we noted in session 1, three
groups of fourteen generations are present, with the exception of

one—the last generation. I noted then that the new believers in Christ are likely implied. Believers are not linked biologically but spiritually. Jesus announced his own relationship to a spiritual family in 12:46-50.

The other prevalent image comes from the Jewish custom of betrothal. When a woman was betrothed (engaged), she left her family of origin to live with the man and his family for a period as long as a year. She joined his family, and she was entrusted to them for the length of the marriage. She bore that family's name and prepared to celebrate the marriage. Breaking the betrothal was tantamount to divorce.

These images of betrothal, engagement, and weddings run throughout Matthew. An angel announces Jesus' birth when a woman and a man are betrothed to one another (1:19). Jesus uses images from weddings to explain the mysteries of the faith family. He likens a believer's life to that of a bride waiting for her groom. Believers prepare for a wedding feast (9:15; 14:16); the king sends invitations for a wedding banquet (22:1); they are prepared for the groom to come at any time (25:1-13).

These two concepts of living as a spiritual family and as a bride betrothed to a groom are held together throughout Matthew. Believers are part of a new spiritual family made possible because of the resurrection of Christ and live in relationship to one another and to God much like a bride prepares for a groom.

The commissioning of the disciples in 28:18-20 makes sense in light of these images. Because the disciples had resurrection faith, they were brought into Jesus' family. They were part of a new generation related spiritually to God and one another. The family had a new name under which they united: "Trinity."

As they moved out and welcomed new members into the family, they used a ritual bath that Jesus experienced in the Jordan River (3:16). The Spirit descended and a voice from heaven identified Jesus' relationship to God. Just as Jesus' baptism expressed the Trinitarian image of the Father, Son, and the Spirit, so the disciples used this name as they moved out into the world. They marked future believers with the family of the trinity (Peterson, *Christ Plays in Ten Thousand Places*, 6-7).

In this faith family, they taught each other how to obey the customs much like an ancient bride prepared to be in a relationship with her husband. In the case of a spiritual family, these instructions are summarized in Matthew 5–7, repeated in the parables, and demonstrated through the activities of Jesus and his followers. They learned to live obediently, not out of duty or obligation, but because they wanted to know the groom better, to understand his family, and to enjoy his continuing presence with them for life. The disciples shared with one another, lived together, learned more about the new family, and discovered the large faith family implied in Matthew 1, which continued through them.

Resurrection Faith

Believers today have resurrection faith. As we noted before, this faith is not belief in the empty tomb. Jesus did not depart from an empty family cemetery. He says farewell from a mountain, the place where God communicated to Moses and where the disciples experienced the risen Christ. Resurrection faith also does not mean simply acknowledging that Jesus came back to life. Even the guards understood that part (see session 10). Resurrection faith experiences the continued presence of Christ in life. Just as the disciples saw (v. 16) and Jesus promised (v. 20), resurrection faith believes in his presence with believers today (Boring, "Matthew," 504).

EXPERIENCE OF THE RISEN CHRIST

The text gives believers several components of resurrection faith that are best visualized as a continuing circle (see Figure 4). Resurrection

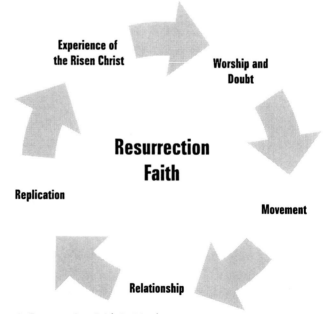

Figure 4. Resurrection Faith in Matthew

faith begins and ends much like this passage, with the experience of the risen Christ.

This faith starts with the personal experience of the risen Christ like the disciples had on the mountain. Each person comes to this experience individually. Just as the disciples personally went to Galilee based on the reports of the women, we believe in the risen Christ by faith.

WORSHIP AND DOUBT

As we noted in session 10, the first response to the risen Christ is worship. But like the disciples who first saw Jesus, even a physical body does not remove all doubts. Worship of Jesus alone is often accompanied by doubt. As Elie Wiesel wrote, "Man comes closer to God by the questions he asks him" (*Night*, 5). These questions, some born out of curiosity and others out of doubt, are often ignored or rejected by others. Believers are taught not to question God or to ask, "Why?" during difficult times.

To ignore the doubts is to ignore the lives of great people like Job, Peter, and Thomas who doubted and opened a doorway to faith through their questions. Part of our relationship with the risen Christ is having the courage to ask questions, reflecting and even disbelieving in moments of uncertainty, and trusting in times when most answers are unavailable. Like a child repeatedly asking if something is real, so our doubts become the doorway through which we walk to worship and experience Christ's presence. We worship even if we doubt.

MOVEMENT

Christ's presence is not stagnant or limited to the location of believers "wherever two or three are gathered." The risen Christ is experienced by moving beyond the safe confines of believers into the nations. Just as Moses and the Israelites moved from Egypt to the Promised Land and Jesus became the new Moses embarking on a journey of forgiveness for the world, so we continue that movement to the people of the nations. The journey does not begin from the religious centers of the world. They, like the ancient Jewish temple, become stagnant, choking off the lives of those who need them the most. The journey begins from the point where we experience the presence of Christ, whether on the mountain or in the valley, and move outward to others.

RELATIONSHIP

The heart of this experience of the risen Christ moves a person toward relationship in a faith family. "Discipling" means inviting someone into the faith family by baptizing, teaching, and modeling this lifestyle to them. We invite, initiate, and train new members of the family of the trinity much like one would prepare a bride to receive a groom. (Incidentally, this is not the only familial/relational metaphor in the New Testament. Paul used the metaphor of adoption.) Believers live in a period of betrothal just as an engaged couple prepares to be married. We await the return of Jesus at the eternal wedding feast. Because no one comes into the spiritual family by birth but by personal decision, we use the symbol of baptism to depict the journey the believer takes from outside the family to inside. Like the name a person is given when he is born physically, the new name of the Trinity indicates our allegiance, loyalty, and spiritual relationship. To learn about our family and how to live as a responsible member of the family, we need instruction and training from one another through speech and life. We remain loyal to the groom not out of a sense of duty (Matt 6) but because we love him and desire to be in relationship with him.

REPLICATION

Our spiritual family does not exist for itself. We are a growing, changing group. The fourteenth generation in the genealogy is incomplete (1:18). As we learn the heritage of our family, and the story that spans from the time of the Hebrew Scriptures (linked symbolically with the genealogy and Jesus as the new Moses) to today, we discover a "story we find ourselves in," to use Brian McLaren's phrase (*The Story We Find Ourselves In* [San Francisco: Jossey-Bass, 2003]).

As Charles Talbert often said in class, the plot of the Bible (and of God's movement in the world) is quite simple:

Creation (of the world)
Crash (through sin)
Covenant
Christ
Church
Consummation

We share this story with others, telling it through speech and life so that others may experience the continued presence of the risen Christ. We enter the story to write the next chapter until the conclusion at the end of the age.

Conclusion

The last word in Matthew is the heart of the story. The book is written because of what happens in the last chapter. Without the resurrection, there is no Gospel and certainly no good news. The author wrote from the perspective of chapter 28, and the audience heard the message in light of what they experienced and lived out as a result of the resurrection.

By the time Matthew was circulated in its present form, all of Paul's letters, the Gospel of Mark, and other oral memories of Jesus' life and ministry had been written. As the generation removed from the eyewitnesses saw their predecessors die and still awaited Jesus' promised return, the book became a way to collect the events, encourage the faithful, and instruct future believers how to imitate the life of their Leader.

What did they imitate? Certainly not Jesus' dress, hairstyle, facial expressions, worship practices, or even eating patterns. We are not given many of these details, nor did they matter to people at that time. Any of the outward imitations led only to Pharisaical hypocrisy.

This generation was concerned little with what could be seen on the outside. They were more interested in people who carried on the behavior of Christ from a heart that reflected ministry to everyone he blessed, from the poor in spirit to the rich tax collector to whom the book is ascribed. From a mountaintop band of eleven, the spiritual family of the church responded by moving out to the nations. Only a resurrection faith could compel this good news to spread.

1. People often remember the last words someone says before he or she dies. In Jesus' case, these are the last words in Matthew's Gospel. What makes these words memorable?

_____

_____

_____

_____

_____

_____

2. What's the difference between a biological family and the family of the Trinity?

_____

_____

_____

_____

_____

_____

3. What does the experience and memory of baptism mean in the life of the believer?

_____

_____

_____

_____

_____

_____

4. Mountains are places where God communicates to people. What are some places in your life where you have experienced the presence of the risen Christ?

_____

_____

_____

_____

_____

_____

5. Resurrection faith is ongoing. There is room for worship and doubt, for moving outward, and for building relationship. How do you cultivate resurrection faith today?

_____
_____
_____
_____
_____
_____

6. What role does doubt play in faith?

_____
_____
_____
_____
_____
_____

7. How do you find yourself in the story of Jesus?

_____
_____
_____
_____
_____
_____

8. Watch this scene from *The Gospel according to St. Matthew* DVD: 1:29:30–1:30:09. The people run to see Jesus share this message. How does their movement demonstrate the movement of the good news?

_____
_____
_____
_____
_____
_____

Bibliography

Banay, Sophia. "World's Most Fun Amusement Parks 2005." Online at http://www.forbes.com/2005/05/26/ cx_sb_0526 feat.html. Accessed 25 April 2007.

Blevins, James L. "Trial of Jesus." *Mercer Dictionary of the Bible.* Edited by Watson Mills. Macon GA: Mercer Press, 1990.

Bonhoeffer, Dietrich. *Life Together.* New York: Harper Collins, 1954; reprint, 1993.

Boring, Eugene. "Matthew." Volume 8. New Interpreter's Bible. Edited by Leander Keck. Nashville: Abingdon, 1995.

Brown, Raymond. *The Birth of the Messiah.* Anchor Bible Reference Library. New York: Doubleday, 1993.

————. *The Death of the Messiah.* Anchor Bible Reference Library. 2 volumes. New York: Doubleday, 1994.

Gaither, Bill. "Family of God." *Bill Gaither.* Published 2005 by Spring House Music Group. Original sound recording made by EMI Christian Music Group (compact disc).

Garland, David. *Reading Matthew: a Literary and Theological Commentary.* Reading the New Testament Series. Edited by Charles Talbert. New York: Crossroad, 1995.

The Gospel according to St. Matthew, DVD. Directed by Pier Paolo Pasolini. 1964. San Diego CA: Legend Films, 2007.

Hanson, K. C., and Douglas E. Oakman. *Palestine in the Time of Jesus: Social Structures and Social Conflicts.* Minneapolis: Fortress Press, 1998.

Hoehner, H. W. "Herodian Dynasty." *Dictionary of Jesus and the Gospels*. Edited by Joel B. Green, et al. Downers Grove IL: Intervarsity Press, 1992.

Hogan, Susan. "A Fresh Sense of God's Love at Christmas." *Dallas Morning News*. 23 December 2000.

Lewis, C. S. *The Chronicles of Narnia: The Lion, the Witch, and the Wardrobe*. New York: Harper Collins, 2006.

Martinson, Roland. "Spiritual but Not Religious: Reaching an Invisible Generation." *Currents in Theology and Mission* 29/5 (October 2002): 1–15.

The Nativity Story, DVD. Directed by Catherine Hardwicke. Los Angeles CA: New Line Entertainment, 2007.

Norris, Kathleen. *Amazing Grace: A Vocabulary of Faith*. New York: Riverhead Books, 1998.

O'Brien, Randall. *I Feel Better All Over than I Do Anywhere Else . . . And Other Stories to Tickle Your Soul*. Macon GA: Peake Road, 1996.

Ortberg, John. *If You Want to Walk on Water, You've Got to Get Out of the Boat*. Grand Rapids: Zondervan, 2001.

Parsons, Mikeal C. "Commentary." Vol. 9 of *Stories about Jesus in the Synoptic Gospels*. Edited by Dennis E. Smith and Michael Williams. Nashville: Abingdon Press, 2005.

The Passion of the Christ, DVD. Directed by Mel Gibson. Hollywood CA: Icon Productions, Twentieth-Century Fox Home Entertainment, 2004.

Peterson, Eugene. *Christ Plays in Ten Thousand Places: A Conversation in Spiritual Theology*. Grand Rapids: Eerdmans, 2006.

Scott, Bernard Brandon. *Hear then the Parable*. Minneapolis: Fortress Press, 1989.

Talbert, Charles. *Reading the Sermon on the Mount*. Grand Rapids: Baker Academic, 2004.

The Visual Bible—Matthew, DVD. Directed by Reghardt van den Bergh. Boca Raton FL: GNN International Corporation and Visual Bible, LLC, 1997.

Wiesel, Elie. *Night*. Translated by Marion Wiesel. New York: Hill and Wang, 1972.

Study the Bible ...

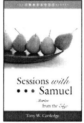

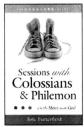
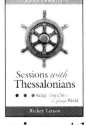

CPSIA information can be obtained
at www.ICGtesting.com
Printed in the USA
FFOW04n2056110518
46625664-48684FF

9 781573 125017